Y0-ABI-401

TENDER
OFFER

TENDER OFFER

The Sneak Attack in Corporate Takeovers

DORMAN L. COMMONS

Foreword by Earl Cheit

University of California Press
Berkeley   Los Angeles   London

University of California Press
Berkeley and Los Angeles, California

University of California Press, Ltd.
London, England

© 1985 by
The Regents of the University of California

Printed in the United States of America
1 2 3 4 5 6 7 8 9

Library of Congress Cataloging in Publication Data
Commons, Dorman L.
   Tender offer.
   Includes index.
   1. Consolidation and merger of corporations—United
States—Case studies.   2. Tender offers (Securities)—
Case studies.   I. Title.
HD2746.5.C65   1985   338.8′3   85-1182
ISBN 0-520-05583-7 (alk. paper)

To Gerry,
who for forty-nine years, forty-four as my wife,
has shared my visions, successes, frustrations, and failures
and has tolerated my imperfections, and whose unflagging support
has always been my most important source of strength.
The "eight days of May" would have been much
more difficult without her.

Contents

Foreword

When a bidding firm makes a tender offer, the target firm is almost certain to change, according to a well-established market maxim. When the chemical-energy corporation Diamond Shamrock of Dallas made a bid for the Natomas Company of San Francisco, an energy-transportation corporation, Natomas changed the way target firms often do—it lost its independence. The struggle that ended when Diamond Shamrock became its new master made news for about ten days.

In the news accounts of that period and in those of other takeover struggles, contests for corporate control are revealed like displays of fireworks. They suddenly burst into view over a full page of newsprint. For a few days following, claims and counter-claims add sparks. The images begin to fade. Then, in a final burst of energy, a decision is announced and the fireworks are over. The whole scene is highly absorbing but not very informative.

When it is over, what do we know? From the formal disclosure required by law, we know the details of the tender offer. News accounts carry the ritual exchanges of the parties, the speculation of financial analysts, and the court maneuvers, if any. And, of course, we know the result: "Big Takeover of S. F. Firm."

What we do not know is how the key issues were approached, what alternatives were considered, how the important decisions were reached, and why.

By dealing with these questions, *Tender Offer* makes a unique contribution to the understanding of the phenomenon of corporate takeovers. Not only does it confirm the market maxim about change in the target firm, but more important, it illuminates the process by which the change occurs. Written from the perspective of the chief executive officer of the target firm, it shows what happens from the time of the tender offer through the hectic days of gathering information, developing a response, and concluding the negotiations—in this case, a total elapsed time of only eight days.

In his skillful reconstruction of those eight days in May 1983, Dormon Commons shows why bidding firms have the advantage, especially when their tender offer comes without warning, putting a small group of executives under a pressing deadline to answer the most complex and fundamental of all business questions: which is better, selling or fighting? In the scramble to formulate an informed answer to that question, goals must be defined, information gathered, alternatives explored, and, if possible, time must be bought. While all this is happening, the ongoing business must be run and a conflict-of-interest situation confronted. Executive career interests and shareholder financial interests are not always the same.

Mr. Commons's account of how he and his colleagues dealt with these issues illuminates still another important proposition about American business: although its language and methods are often highly rational, its impelling motives and underlying drive are those of risk and adventure. Computer models helped provide Natomas with information about when fighting should give way to selling. But the defense strategy was shaped and executed with the skills on which generals and poker players depend.

The urge to merge is old and well established in American business. The first wave of mergers occurred in the mid-1890s, a product of horizontal combinations and changes in the nation's capital market. Merger movements also occurred in the 1920s and again in the 1960s and early 1970s.

Today American business is once again creating a wave of mergers and acquisitions. Just how big a wave can be judged from figures gathered by W. T. Grimm and Company, a firm that specializes in this information. It tabulates every publicly reported transfer of at least 10 percent of ownership of a company's assets or equity where the sum exceeds $500,000. Each transfer of control is called a "transaction." In 1983, 2,533 such transactions took place. Diamond Shamrock's takeover of Natomas was one of them.

Although 2,533 transactions is a large number (about ten for every working day), it is still well below the record year of 1969, when the tabulated total reached 6,017. Yet the current merger and acquisition activity has raised serious public policy questions, concerns as strong as any in recent history. The issue has been the subject of special hearings by the Securities and Exchange Commission, committees of Congress, and academic and business conferences. Is the market for corporate control producing a paper entrepreneurialism whose costs exceed its benefits? This question has stirred such widespread interest that in 1985 the members of President Reagan's Council of Economic Advisors prepared a special section of their annual report on this issue.

What has propelled this subject into national attention are the techniques used to finance and carry out takeovers, some of the tactics used to resist them, and, above all, the dollar size of this new merger activity. Although the numbers of transactions are still not as large as in the late 1960s, the dollar value of corporate assets changing hands is far greater. In 1983, control over $73.1 billion changed hands, Natomas included. The comparable figure for 1969 (measured in 1983 dollars) is $58.8 billion. For 1984 the estimate is that $132.6 billion changed hands. The average value of mergers and acquisitions in 1981–1984 was about 50 percent greater (in constant dollars) than those in the late 1960s and early 1970s, the peak of recent merger activity.

In reviewing his own experiences as part of the larger merger phenomenon, Mr. Commons raises the key question: do the costs exceed the benefits? At present a lively literature on the market for corporate control says "no," based on the behavior of the stock market. Takeovers are beneficial, the argument goes, because studies show that the aggregate net change in the value of the bidding and target companies' shares is positive.* Although Mr. Commons has solid personal and professional reasons to agree with this conclusion in his own case, his broader concerns, which are not reflected in the short-term behavior of stock prices, lead him to express ambivalent feelings about the outcome.

What are the effects of takeovers on communities? Are the companies more efficient and productive? Is the economy generally stronger? Answers to these questions must await careful case-by-case research on the actual impact of mergers. Already there are enough individual observations to suggest that the longer-term answers may be less enthusiastic about the results than the observations that rely only on short-term stock market evaluations.

One case worth following will be that of Diamond Shamrock of Dallas. In April 1985, when Unocal, the holding company for Union Oil of California, was a target company in an unfriendly takeover bid, it was widely rumored that

*Readers of *Tender Offer* who wish to examine this argument should consult the *Economic Report of the President* (Washington, D.C.: U.S. Government Printing Office, 1985), pp. 187–217, and Michael C. Jensen, "Takeovers: Folklore and Science," *Harvard Business Review* 62 (November–December 1984): 109–121.

another company was available for purchase by Unocal to give it a debt burden that would make it an unattractive target. That company, according to press reports, was Diamond Shamrock. Its shares were selling at about 20 percent below their market price at the time of the tender offer that resulted in this book.

Collectors of irony will especially appreciate the fact that at its annual meeting in May 1985, Diamond Shamrock asked its shareholders to approve several anti-takeover measures, including by-law amendments that would stagger terms of directors, ban payments of greenmail, and thwart two-tiered offers. In its proxy materials Diamond Shamrock explained that these measures were intended to protect shareholders from takeover tactics that were often disruptive and inequitable.

Earl F. Cheit
Edgar F. Kaiser Professor of Business and Public Policy
University of California, Berkeley

Preface

This is a very personal narrative from the point of view of the chief executive officer of Natomas Company, a San Francisco–based corporation targeted for an unfriendly takeover by Diamond Shamrock of Dallas, Texas. I have tried to be completely faithful to the facts as I recall them and to convey the trauma as well as the excitement of a modern corporate battle. I have made no attempt to represent the point of view of Diamond Shamrock's management. What led them to choose Natomas Company? Why did they not approach me before launching the tender offer attack? What was their rationale in agreeing to the final terms? I know only what they stated publicly and can but surmise what their other reasons might have been. I am sure that Bill Bricker, Diamond Shamrock's chief executive officer, would see the events of May 1983 in a significantly different light. I hope my story will be of interest and value to the managements of public companies in the United States and to their stockholders.

Natomas, like any modern corporation, is indebted for its success, if it has any, to its management team and organization. Both in building the company and in dealing with our final crisis, Natomas, its shareholders, and I were exceptionally well served by a competent entrepreneurial, if sometimes fractious, top management team and one of the finest groups of managers and technicians I have ever seen assembled.

I am eternally grateful for the guidance and support from Ken Reed, Bruce Seaton, Charlie Lee, Mick Seidl, Joe Mandel, and a host of others who shared that experience. I owe a special tribute to Dean Lewis and Dante Lembi, whose contributions to Natomas were vitally important but whose deaths robbed them of that final hour. Finally, I wish to offer thanks to Michael Stone of World College West, whose aid and expertise in organizing, researching, preliminary drafting, and constructive suggestions were of such help in preparing this narrative.

Introduction

The *San Francisco Examiner*'s headline for May 31, 1983, read, "Big Takeover of S.F. Firm." The next day the *Wall Street Journal* proclaimed, "Natomas Merger with Diamond Shamrock Set," while the *New York Daily News* announced— *not* on the society page—"Diamond, Natomas to Wed." Behind the stark headlines lay the most dramatic week of my life and a classic example of the recent fundamental restructuring of the way American businesses do business.

Only nine days earlier I had learned that the Diamond Shamrock Corporation, a Dallas firm about which I knew practically nothing, was launching a bid for control of Natomas, the billion-dollar-plus company that I had served as president and chief executive officer for nearly ten years. The ensuing week found me on the battlefield that has come to characterize contemporary American business. Even the casual reader of any daily newspaper's business page has doubtless noticed something afoot: oil companies prospecting for each other's shareholders rather than for new fields; liquor distillers and chemical companies fighting for control of energy companies; multibillion-dollar mergers; the new argot of the new dealermaker, with his "white knights," "greenmail," and "golden parachutes." But perhaps only a person who has been in business his whole adult life, as I have, and has been involved in mergers and acquisitions for more than thirty years can really appreciate how much has changed in a very short time.

Our eight-day skirmish offers one glimpse of the new corporate warfare. By the week's end, the Natomas Company, an independent entity since the California gold rush, was destined to merge. Had we "lost" our battle? Not completely. The corporate terrain had changed irreversibly, but there were very tangible gains for our shareholders, at least in the short-term. No one, not even management, expected a resolution, especially one so favorable, in such a short time. Natomas's common shareholders emerged on May 31 with a premium for their stock double that which they had been offered a week earlier. They would receive securities in two potentially strong companies rather than one weakened firm, and every non-executive Natomas employee—without access to the executive suite—received monetary considerations unprecedented in such a takeover.

That week in May was one of corporate tension and personal revelation, a reminder that the generalizations of business school textbooks can never wholly describe the dynamics that emerge when business principles mix with human needs and egos. The success we achieved was due to many factors: preparations made months before we had ever heard of Diamond Shamrock's interest in Natomas; a "defense team" ready for mobilization within hours; computer modeling of every aspect of our complex company; a set of flexible strategies responsive to the multiple goals we had set for ourselves; our ability to analyze the worth of our company quickly and the courage to walk away from an inadequate offer.

Consideration of our preparations and strategies and the lessons we learned in our battle for survival may be helpful to others facing the same threat. But a close look at the anatomy of this corporate defense may leave others a bit disquieted, just as I am, and with many unanswered questions.

Given the circumstances, I believe that we did well, at least in the short run, for our shareholders and employees. The officers of Diamond Shamrock apparently felt they had also done well by their constituencies. But is either company better off in the long term? Is the corporate economy or our society as a whole well served by the new warfare and the time and expense devoted to waging it? Who profits, finally, and who pays? To examine these questions, I look backward to and forward from that critical day in May when I first knew that my life and that of my company were about to be changed forever.

· 1 ·

The Battle Is Joined

I had spent all day Friday, May 20, in court in Houston. As chief executive officer (CEO) of the Natomas Company, I was testifying in a complicated, frustrating case involving a suit and countersuit over contractual rights concerning two of our subsidiaries. Trial on substantive matters was still months away; the court was now simply considering the legal interpretation of a variety of documents and wanted my testimony. It was not the way I would have chosen to enjoy spending a spring day.

When I left the courtroom, I was handed a note that Charlie Lee, our senior vice-president for finance, was trying to reach me from San Francisco with an urgent message. Charlie reported that one of our directors, Forrest Shumway, had called to say that he had it on good authority that someone—he wasn't quite sure who—was set to drop a tender offer on Natomas at the end of business that day.

A tender offer, though perhaps much desired in affairs of the heart, is anything but sweet news in business, where it frequently means a cash or securities bid for a company, made directly to the company's shareholders without consultation or cooperation from its management, often as a prelude to a wholesale takeover of the company.

That figured. The end of the day on Friday, after the

stock market has closed for the week, when a company is least likely to be prepared to respond quickly, is the typical time for unsolicited, unfriendly tenders. A Friday move also allows the tendering company the weekend, while the market is closed, to prepare its assault. It can purchase advertisements for the Monday morning *Wall Street Journal*, print offers to purchase and other materials to be sent to shareholders—all without worrying about leaks of information or other strategic impediments.

Besides, it had been that kind of week, beginning with an emergency trip to the hospital the previous Sunday. My wife Gerry and I had scheduled a piano recital in our home that afternoon, but I had spent it instead attending to my first attack of kidney stones. The stone, and the crisis, passed on Monday, and I flew to New York and then Houston for meetings. Now I was sitting in the airport in Houston trying to get a commercial flight home; a wayward fuel truck had disabled our company plane during a freak cyclone at the airport the night before.

Takeover rumors were nothing new. The previous two weeks had seen persistent and inflated buying in Natomas stock: 685,000 shares on May 10 (compared to 200,000 to 300,000 shares a day the week before); 618,000 shares on May 11; 573,000 shares on Monday, May 16; nearly 804,000 shares on Thursday, May 19; 1,178,500 shares on Friday, May 20. The price had climbed steadily, from $15.50 a share to $18.50, a 20 percent increase in two weeks.

For a variety of reasons I felt the company had long been undervalued by the market. And rumors had flown for years, with attendant spurts and slips in stock prices. In recent years prospective suitors (the colorful language is about the only thing "tender" about a tender offer) included Marathon Oil, Occidental Petroleum, and The Signal Companies. In February our stock had soared precipitously during a few days of heavy trading, only to fall back just as quickly when the rumors subsided.

Signal, which already held a 12.5 percent interest in Natomas, figured prominently in rumors again in March 1983, along with a new name, Diamond Shamrock Corporation of Dallas. Speculators started buying stock on the strength of the rumors or on inside information—one can never be sure which, especially since we learned later that Diamond Shamrock had been actively considering Natomas as a takeover candidate at just that time. When the rumors faded, the stock lost 2¾ points in one day, with 1,377,100 shares changing hands.

I had been concerned about the movement and had checked regularly with our specialist on the floor of the New York Stock Exchange. He reported that there were takeover rumors of the same sort we had heard before, but nothing he could pin down. Although I had gone to New York the previous week for another purpose, while there I did meet with our investment bankers and lawyers to review plans in case the rumors should prove to have any substance.

Beyond that, there wasn't much to do. Sometimes I am sure Wall Street runs just on rumor, but sometimes someone knows—or guesses—that something is in the offing and tries to turn a profit on a pending merger or takeover. Of course, the rules of the stock exchanges and the Securities and Exchange Commission (SEC) strictly prohibit trading on the basis of privileged information, but those rules are frequently flouted, and insider trading remains one of the most troublesome matters for the market. And frankly, the problem seems intractable since the preparation of any tender offer or merger requires numerous participants: officers of the companies themselves, investment bankers, law firms, public relations people, clerks, messengers—

you name it—as well as the people they talk to every day. A supervisor for a financial printing company that prepares the documentation accompanying tender offers was recently convicted of leaking tips about upcoming acquisitions to stockbrokers, who turned the information into more than $500,000 in illegal profits. Despite the potential criminal liabilities, unauthorized disclosures occur and word does get out. In our case, the New York Stock Exchange investigated but, as far as I know, never found evidence of anything illicit. Yet someone, through luck or inside information, made a lot of money buying Natomas stock before the merger bid was made public.

I took the commercial flight back to San Francisco, and Gerry and I went out to our home in Marin County for the weekend. Nothing of consequence happened Saturday. We spent our time relaxing, doing odd jobs, reading, and listening to music.

Sunday afternoon Jamie Campbell, who until recently had been head of our public relations department, called Mary O'Neill, my executive assistant. (Mary fought a tenacious if somewhat ineffective battle against being referred to as my secretary.) Jamie had been called by a *Wall Street Journal* reporter based in San Francisco for response to a rumor that Diamond Shamrock was planning to mount a tender offer for Natomas the next day. Mary suggested that Jamie phone me, and I told him I would take a call from the reporter.

The reporter stated that he had it "on good authority" that Diamond Shamrock would begin a tender offer Monday morning for 51 percent of Natomas's outstanding shares at $23.00 a share, or about $700 million in all. If successful, according to the reporter, Diamond intended to effect a merger by offering to exchange the remaining 49 percent of Natomas for Diamond Shamrock stock at a ratio of 1 share of Natomas for 0.92 shares of Diamond. With Diamond then selling at about $25 the exchange would yield $23 for each Natomas share.

I asked the reporter where he had received this information, which seemed extremely detailed for a mere rumor. He said the story was being widely reported on the East Coast; I learned subsequently that Diamond had purchased advertisements for Monday in both the *Wall Street Journal* and the *New York Times*, and that the *Times* had already gone to press with the story. The reporter asked for a comment. I expressed considerable skepticism about the story's accuracy. I had not heard from anybody at Diamond Shamrock, and the previous week's heavy volume of trading in Natomas and the specter of insider trading seemed to support my doubts. "If anyone were going to make a tender offer for us in the face of all the movement in Natomas stock that occurred last week, they should have their heads examined," I told him. "If they do move it should certainly interest the Securities and Exchange Commission."

Well, maybe they *should* have had their heads examined, but it turned out that Diamond Shamrock was preparing a tender offer, on precisely the terms outlined by the reporter. I received another call a few minutes later from Tully Friedman, the San Francisco managing director of Salomon Brothers, one of our investment bankers. Their manager of mergers and acquisitions, Jay Higgins, had been called in New York by Marty Siegel, who held the similar position with Kidder, Peabody & Co. Siegel was calling "as a matter of courtesy" to say that his firm had been retained by Diamond Shamrock to represent them as investment bankers in the tender offer.

This courtesy call was one of the ceremonial "nice gestures" in the corporate ritual we were about to perform. Marty Siegel also said that William Bricker, chairman of the board and chief executive officer of Diamond Shamrock, "had been trying, as a matter of courtesy, to reach Mr. Commons all week" to inform me of his intent.

The tribal rituals of the corporate world have always fascinated me. I suspect they are rather similar to the rules of warfare. (In fact, Karl von Clausewitz makes the explicit comparison between business competition and warfare in his classic nineteenth-century study, *On War*.) I've always found the notion of rules for warfare—etiquette for people bent on each other's destruction—to be curious. Somehow we human beings love to formalize our behavior, even in such disparate activities as love and war. I suspected the relationship I was about to engage in with Mr. Bricker was more likely to resemble the latter than the former, but in any event, I found it hard to consider his call to be much of a courtesy, and he obviously hadn't tried very hard to reach me; the reporters certainly had had no trouble accomplishing that.

No matter. The gauntlet was down and the game, or battle, was on.

· 2 ·

The Defense Team

As recently as five or six years ago, the chances of a company with a net worth over $1 billion being taken over had seemed extremely slim. Then came the Reagan administration and a new attitude toward antitrust regulation. Previous administrations, Republican and Democratic alike for thirty years, had demonstrated vigilant concern about business combinations that *might* reduce competition. The Reagan administration relaxed this concern and virtually abandoned size as a criterion in antitrust determinations. The floodgates on mergers were about to open. Conoco, a hundred-year-old, $7 billion firm that had previously seemed invulnerable, sought a "safe haven" with Dupont, which outbid Seagram and Mobil. (Many factors make one potential partner more attractive than another; in this case, Conoco's management preferred Dupont partly because Dupont's executive suites, unlike those at Mobil, were not already populated with executives able to run an oil company.) It soon became evident that no company, no matter how large, was safe from the threat of an imposed merger.

Fortunately, we had felt for some time that we were vulnerable to an unsolicited tender offer, and we had made preparations to quickly evaluate any offer and ensure that our shareholders would get the best possible deal. After

7

our telephone conversation Friday, Charlie Lee and I activated an alert system we had designed to enable us to locate the players we would need. Sunday afternoon we got to work. Joe Mandel, our general counsel, Ken Reed, our vice-chairman, and Bruce Seaton, our president, were all in Jakarta tending to business concerning our Indonesian holdings. I asked Charlie to arrange for their immediate return home.

Then I called the firm we had already selected to lead our legal defense. We knew we would need good local counsel (we later retained Morrison and Foerster, in San Francisco, who performed admirably), but we would also need assistance from one of the Wall Street firms that had developed a specialty in mergers and acquisitions.

The laws covering takeovers and mergers are enormously complicated, and any slip-up can provide an opening for either an offensive or a defensive gambit. When making our contingency preparations against unsolicited takeover attempts, I had interviewed the principals of two New York law firms noted for their expertise in defending corporations against hostile takeovers.

In 1982 Dean Lewis, who was then our general counsel, and I had decided to retain Skadden, Arps, Slate, Meagher & Flom, whose defense team would be led by Joseph Flom, the rumpled, pipe-smoking, brilliant senior partner and the dean of lawyers in this field. Few recent major corporate takeover battles have been fought without Joe and his minions appearing either for the offense or the defense, and he has had remarkable success in both positions. However, also of note, Joe Flom has almost invariably found himself opposed by the New York firm of Wachtell, Lipton, Rosen and Katz, with its senior partner Martin Lipton as Joe's very canny and effective opponent. I was not surprised to learn that afternoon that Marty Lipton would be representing Diamond Shamrock.

Another group of important players in these transactions are the investment bankers. Along with specialty lawyers, they help lay out defensive tactics, based on their ability to analyze a company and evaluate its options. Among their many contributions, they offer opinions on the appropriateness of the original and subsequent offers, help evaluate the company's worth, and advise management and directors on the likely success of strategies such as the company's attempting to buy back its own shares. Investment bankers also use their contacts to seek alternative merger partners (the "white knights") who might pay a higher price or be willing to offer better conditions.

Every major investment banking firm in the country has a department that makes its living and earns its reputation by promoting or defending against mergers and acquisitions. Certainly not all mergers are unfriendly, but bankers capable of mounting a strong offense or defense in an unfriendly merger are well compensated for their efforts, and deservedly so.

The investment banker must know a company well in order to make rapid and accurate assessments. Fortunately, we had three firms in an excellent position to help us. Earlier in May, we had gone to the public market with the sale of 3.5 million shares of Natomas common stock. This issue had been underwritten by Salomon Brothers, Lazard Frères and Company, and Warburg, Paribas, Becker. In underwriting a company's offering, investment bankers guarantee the company an agreed-upon price, then resell the shares to their own customers. The underwriters thus play a major role in setting the price of the new shares and accept responsibility for selling a substantial portion of the shares themselves, while arranging the distribution of the balance of shares to be marketed by other investment bankers and brokers. The underwriters are also required by law to complete due diligence work, putting their own names and reputations behind the accuracy of the factual statements in an offering's prospectus.

Beyond the legal requirements, self-interest dictates that investment bankers not commit themselves to an offering nor tout it to their customers until they thoroughly know a company and its prospects. If the shares do not sell at the asking price, the underwriters are stuck with them; if the shares sell but prove to be a poor investment, an investment house loses its customers' confidence and sometimes its customers. Having managed our offering, Salomon Brothers and Lazard Frères had become well acquainted with Natomas, and their representatives had been to Indonesia only a few weeks earlier to review our overseas operations.

Though several firms were well qualified to help coordinate our defense, I decided on this Sunday afternoon to rely on Lazard Frères and on Salomon. A corporation's relationship with an investment banker is a highly personal as well as professional matter. During a merger or takeover battle, a CEO must frequently rely on the judgment of an investment banker and has to have one who merits complete trust. In turn, if a deal is consummated, the investment banker stands to earn fees that can run to millions of dollars, depending on the nature and details of the final agreement (or lack of agreement, in the case of a firm brought on specifically to help resist an offer). Thus a CEO has to have absolute confidence that his or her banker is recommending the deal that is best for the company, not just the one that will generate the highest bankers' fees.

Through the years I have had the chance to meet and evaluate a number of the best investment bankers in the country. One name high on any list of leading bankers is Felix Rohatyn, managing partner of Lazard Frères in New York. Not only has he been highly successful in leading that firm in the private sector, but also he is generally credited (quite rightly, I believe) as the chief architect of the plan that saved New York City from bankruptcy. Felix and I had become good friends, partly through our mutual if peripheral interest in Democratic party politics. I had come to implicitly trust his judgment, his intellectual honesty, and his candor. I also knew and respected Jim Glanville, another senior partner at Lazard Frères, who is regarded as one of the most knowledgeable oil investment bankers in the country.

Salomon Brothers had also been one of our investment banking firms for a number of years and had managed a number of public issues for us. John Gutfreund, the affable, smiling, but hard-driving managing partner of that firm in New York, had also become a friend, as had Tully Friedman, their managing director in San Francisco. I turned readily to them in this crisis.

As part of our preparations for a possible hostile takeover attempt on Natomas, we had periodically rehearsed, refined, and modified our strategy in concert with our investment bankers and with Joe Flom and his associates at Skadden, Arps. But even with planning, the real event is traumatic and the outcome uncertain. Of course, all the planning and dry runs in the world cannot duplicate the shock of the real thing, but more important, both law and duty limit any management's ability to insulate itself from offers, hostile or otherwise. A company's officers and directors are pledged to act in the best interests of the stockholders, a responsibility that precludes any knee-jerk rejection of a takeover offer. A management or board of directors that devises schemes to protect against any and all offers is liable to find itself on the defensive in court against a stockholders' suit.

Sunday afternoon suddenly became very busy, and my adrenalin kept pace. The laws concerning tender offers put a premium on rapid response, so we couldn't afford to wait even until Monday. Charlie Lee, the only other senior officer in town, and I started dividing up the work. He began gathering the Natomas team, while I tried to contact our local and New York associates. Tully Friedman arranged for a team from their New York mergers and acquisitions group, headed by Jay Higgins, to be on their way to San Francisco the next morning. So far so good. Felix Rohatyn was somewhere between his country home and his New York apartment; I left word both places. Then, our first snag.

I called Stuart Shapiro, a Skadden, Arps partner I had seen in New York a few weeks earlier, and suggested that he have a team fly out to San Francisco the next day. He agreed. But he called back a short time later to suggest that they "might have a problem" and would get back to me in the morning.

"A problem" turned out to be more than that. Skadden, Arps had previously represented Diamond Shamrock and was on retainer. The next morning, though, Joe Flom assured me he would be with us. The retainer agreements written by Skadden, Arps had anticipated this possibility and specified that if two of the firm's clients contended against each other, the client needing defense would receive the assistance. However, because of agreements and other work they had done for Diamond Shamrock, Joe concluded that he could not actually litigate on our behalf or lead any attack on Diamond Shamrock. In the event of litigation, we would have to retain San Francisco counsel. He could, however, advise us on any negotiations with Diamond Shamrock and on our obligations in responding to the offer.

I then remembered that at one time Dean Lewis and I had flirted with the idea of attempting to deny potential aggressors the choicest weapons by retaining both Skadden, Arps and Wachtell, Lipton—as it turned out Diamond Shamrock had done. (What a waste of money that would have been!) But we had concluded that there were other competent firms in the field and that we could never "drink the ocean" by retaining them all. In hindsight, I think we made the right decision, although maybe for the wrong reasons. We had held similar discussions through the years with a variety of investment bankers, including Kidder, Peabody, who had approached us some two years earlier about the possibility of retaining them for defense against potential takeovers. Nothing had come of those discussions, but I've since wondered whether our talks might not have alerted them to Natomas's vulnerability when their own client, Diamond Shamrock, came seeking acquisitions.

I also called Tom Neville, our vice-president for corporate development, and asked him to start digging immediately: What was the basis of Diamond Shamrock's interest in Natomas? How badly did they want the merger? What kind of record did they have? Would they be good managers of Natomas's assets if they did effect the merger? Were there grounds for recommending that our stockholders oppose the merger? Was Diamond at all vulnerable to a lawsuit that could delay the bid? What else could he find out, and how soon? About all we knew at that point was that Diamond Shamrock, a Dallas-based company, had begun in chemicals and only recently shifted its emphasis toward energy. Their name had surfaced as a rumored corporate suitor during recent weeks, but so had a dozen other names. We needed to know volumes, but we had only days. Fortunately, I had been diligent in one of my most important jobs as a CEO: I had hired people I knew I could trust to do an excellent job. In this case I knew I could rely on Tom to make the most of the little time we had. His first briefing paper reached my desk the next morning.

If the battle turned into one of public perception or into a struggle for the votes of stockholders, we would need a strong public relations firm. After trying unsuccessfully most of Sunday afternoon, I finally reached the New York manager of Hill and Knowlton, Dick Chaney, whom I had known for a number of years. He would have a senior man in our office the next day.

Tully Friedman called. Their New York team would be on the way first thing in the morning. Did I want to take a call from William Bricker? At this point my initial sense of shock turned to anger. Diamond had already made its move; they were going after Natomas without warning. Why in hell should I take a call? We agreed that nothing would be accomplished by taking a call that evening; we'd wait for Monday. Tully also reported that a formal letter from Diamond Shamrock outlining their terms would be delivered to me Monday. I did take a call from the *San Francisco Chronicle*. I had not seen Diamond Shamrock's letter and therefore had no comment, but I affirmed that the tender offer was clearly "unfriendly."

I called Mary O'Neill to begin changing my plans and appointments. A three-week trip to the Far East, including Indonesia, then on to Europe, was to have begun the day after our Board of Directors meeting, scheduled for June 1. The meeting was suddenly likely to be much more important than we had anticipated. The trip had to be canceled; I would not be leaving San Francisco for a while. Although my senior executives could not make it back from Jakarta before Tuesday, a great many steps would have to be initiated before then, using whoever was available.

Gerry and I decided to go back to our apartment in San Francisco, where I would be close to the office in the morning. By doing so, I missed Felix Rohatyn's call, but I caught him early Monday morning. Back in San Francisco, after a couple of hours in which I alerted as many of the seventeen members of our Board of Directors as I could reach, I went to bed, but not to dream—nor to sleep either for that matter. My gut was tied in a knot, but all my senses were alert. My mind raced from thoughts of possible defensive moves to contemplating how drastically my world had changed in just a few hours. During the night my anger drained away. There wasn't time for me to indulge my personal responses—I had to direct all my energy toward the battle ahead.

· 3 ·

Timetables

Monday morning we began to work in earnest. Tom Neville continued digging for more information on Diamond Shamrock. Charlie Lee confirmed that the group from Jakarta would be back Tuesday morning. I received an interesting, and very heartening, call from Sam Armacost, president and chief executive officer of Bank of America. Sam wanted me to know that their resources were available and that they were prepared to help us. We had already established for other purposes about $600 million in credit with Bank of America as one of our lead banks. We did not yet know how much more we might need, but it certainly meant a great deal to me to know we had friends in the financial community. And several defensive ploys—buying back our own stock or engaging Diamond in a bidding war, adding a subsidiary that would make Natomas less attractive or create antitrust problems for Diamond Shamrock, or a number of variations on any of these—would require substantial financial backing.

That day I also called the rest of our outside directors, all of whom assured me that they considered the Diamond Shamrock tender offer inadequate. I also gave them a brief idea of the defensive steps we would be exploring. But Forrest Shumway was in Paris on business; he was not only a director but also CEO of The Signal Companies, our largest shareholder with over a 12.5 percent interest. Signal's stance in the coming battle was critical.

Forrest had alerted us on Friday before he left for Paris to the persistent rumors about a takeover. He was supportive but clear: He felt $23 a share for Natomas stock was too low, but at $30 a share, he added, "I may have trouble keeping my directors from accepting the offer." Obviously, he and his Signal Board of Directors wouldn't want to be left in the position of having all their Natomas shares subject to the second-tier transaction—that is, refuse to tender their shares for cash only to be forced later to exchange them for Diamond shares once Diamond acquired 51 percent of Natomas. His comment was not one I would forget.

And I talked strategy several times Monday with Felix Rohatyn and with Tully Friedman and John Gutfreund. Our first task was to inform ourselves about the deadlines under which we had to operate, particularly those mandated by securities laws and SEC regulations.

A word of background might be helpful here. The corporate culture of the United States, with its encouragement of free competition, including even government intercession to promote that competition, is unique in the world. SEC regulations regarding corporate warfare are analogous to the Geneva Convention treaties, intended to regulate warfare between nations. Just as the Geneva Convention has much to say about the treatment of civilians and noncombatants, the SEC directs much of its attention not to protecting the battling corporations but to safeguarding the shareholders threatened by the crossfire.

The SEC was created by the Securities Exchange Act of 1934, part of the general overhaul of stock trading practices in the wake of the abuses that helped precipitate the 1929 crash. The SEC oversees the issuance and sale of new stock, for instance, by requiring public disclosure about the ownership, assets, liabilities, and previous performance of a company and its officers and principal shareholders. The due diligence investigations our investment bankers had completed to satisfy the SEC regulations prior to our common stock offering would stand us in good stead now, giving our bankers a head start toward helping us quickly evaluate Natomas's present worth and prospects. Meanwhile, we would be combing the disclosure statements Diamond Shamrock had filed with the SEC. Any omissions or actionable statements could block or slow the progress of the tender offer.

Many of the most relevant SEC regulations for us at this point derived from Public Law 90-439 of July 29, 1968 (better known as the Williams Act) and its subsequent refinements. The legislation had first been introduced in 1965 by Senator Harrison Williams, who represented New Jersey from 1959 until his resignation in 1982 after running afoul of the Abscam investigation. Williams's bill amended the Securities Exchange Act specifically to regulate tender offers more closely.

Until then, a shareholder was much more likely to receive a take-it-or-leave-it tender offer from a potential buyer, often with little chance to evaluate either the buyer or the offer. The "Saturday Night Special" offer (so called because it was made over the weekend, when the stock market was closed and the target company was not in a position to respond) would specify terms for a quick sale. For example, stockholders would receive an offer of $30 a share for stock whose market price was $20—providing they tendered immediately. In order to discourage investors from waiting for any better deal, the offer applied only to the first 20 percent tendered, with the price dropping after that, or even dropping for shareholders who waited more than three days to respond. But some shareholders accepted the $30 offer, only to find that a few days later the offer had been increased or a second bidder was offering an even higher price.

Meanwhile, the company making the tender offer did not have to disclose its reasons for purchasing the stock: whether as an investment, as a prelude to taking over management of the company, for purposes of liquidation, or whatever. Thus those shareholders whose interest extended beyond immediate stock prices to concern with the company's management, product, or likely future earnings were unable to assess the probable impact of the purchase. In some instances, stockholders could not even identify who the offerers were or whom they represented.

In language that he later muted somewhat, Senator Williams argued, "We have seen proud old companies reduced to corporate shells after white-collar pirates have seized control with funds from sources which are unknown in many cases, then sold or traded the best assets, later to split up most of the loot among themselves."* The primary aim of the Williams Act was to require "full and fair disclosure for the benefit of investors." The original language applied to cash offers for securities; it was amended in 1970 to also include offers involving the exchange of securities. Subsequent interpretations by the courts have held that the act was not intended to encourage tender offers nor to provide the management of a target company with defensive tools. Nor was it intended, according to court interpretations, to help shareholders by artificially forcing up the market, but only to assure the investors sufficient information and time to make a rational decision.†

Several of the provisions and later amendments to the

* Quoted by Earl W. Kintner, *Primer on the Law of Mergers: A Guide for the Businessman* (New York: Macmillan, 1973), p. 72.

† See, for example, *Piper* v. *Chris-Craft Industries, Inc.*, 430 U.S. 1 (1977); *Rondeau* v. *Mosinee Paper Corp.*, 422 U.S. 49 (1975); *Kennecott Corporation* v. *Smith*, 637 F.2d 181 (3d Cir. 1980).

Williams Act stipulated ground rules for our upcoming skirmish. The tendering institution is required, first, to file statements identifying itself, its recent transactions, any civil proceedings concerning securities law violations in which it has been involved during the preceding five years, the number of shares it already owns of the company being purchased, the source and amount of the funds it plans to use (and whether it will need to borrow those funds), the purpose of its proposed purchase, the plans it has to liquidate, merge, or make other major changes in the corporation whose shares it seeks, and so on. All this information would be important to us as we evaluated the adequacy of Diamond Shamrock's offer and looked for any legal grounds for stopping or delaying the tender.

To prevent Saturday Night Specials, the Williams Act requires that tender offers must remain open for a minimum period of time, allowing shareholders the opportunity to consider the offer and wait for a better one. By law, the Diamond Shamrock offer had to remain open for twenty business days, or until midnight, June 20. These same rules applied to defensive responses by Natomas. If we were to turn around and make a counteroffer for Diamond Shamrock's stock (the "Pac-Man maneuver") or attempt to buy some other company in order to complicate matters for Diamond, Diamond could still acquire control of Natomas while our counteroffer was caught up in the twenty-day holding period.

However, SEC rules permit a company to make an offer for its own shares subject to only a ten-day holding period. If we chose to make a self-tender within ten days, we could start buying shares while Diamond Shamrock was still constrained by the holding period that applies to outside offers. But during the wait-and-see period, even though they could do nothing to stop anyone who decided to tender to us, they would probably crank up their public relations machinery, making promises to sweeten the offer for Natomas shareholders who were willing to wait. To further complicate matters, if a third company chose to enter the fray (as a Natomas ally or simply as an interested buyer) with its own tender offer for Natomas stock, then the period for withdrawal of shares tendered to but not yet purchased by Diamond would be automatically extended for ten more business days.

We had only ten business days for sure, then, to initiate any offer for our own shares if we hoped to purchase them while Diamond remained hamstrung by the waiting period, or twenty business days to develop a defense or find someone willing to make a counteroffer more appealing than Diamond's. Of course, another buyer might enter the bidding during this period, but that was out of our control.

June 20 also marked the end of the *proration period* mandated by the Williams Act in order to protect investors from being pressured to tender prematurely by threats to change the terms of the offer. During the proration period of twenty business days, all shares tendered have to be treated equally: If more than the number of shares sought in the initial offer are tendered during the proration period and if the offerer chooses not to buy the additional shares, then purchases have to be made on a pro rata basis from each shareholder who responded to the tender. In our case, for example, Diamond had offered to buy up to 30.4 million shares of Natomas stock—51 percent of the outstanding common stock—at $23 a share. But if 40 million shares were tendered and Diamond chose to limit its purchase to the 30 million shares it had first sought, then Diamond would buy three out of every four shares tendered by each shareholder during the proration period. So, a shareholder tendering 1,000 shares by June 20 would receive from Diamond $23 a share for 750 shares and would retain the remaining 250 shares. Were Diamond to increase its offering price during the proration period, then it would have to purchase all shares tendered, both before and after the increase, at the new, higher price. Twenty working days—four calendar weeks—marked the time frame within which we would have to maneuver.

The Williams Act further protects shareholders by providing them with the option of withdrawing tendered shares within a specified period should they reconsider or receive a better offer. Natomas shareholders tendering to Diamond would have until midnight, June 13, or until ten business days after the commencement of another offer (whichever was later) to withdraw their shares. That meant we really had just three weeks to maneuver. Practically, however, our work would need to be done in even less time than that.

The Williams Act does not require a target company to respond immediately in any way to a tender offer. However, if the company does choose to advise its stockholders to accept or reject an offer, or to opt for an alternative, then the company is required by the SEC to advise shareholders of the position of its Board of Directors within ten business days of the original offer. Moreover, upon electing to respond, the company is required to file with the SEC a Schedule 14D Statement. Along with routine information about the company, the 14D Statement must detail recent trading activity in the company's stock and provide information about any solicitation and the reasons for the solicitation or recommendation. The 14D Statement must also include any "material facts" regarding the company's response to the tender offer, including financing arrangements and alternative proposals it has received or would accept. At one time a company could simply tell its stockholders, "We regard the offer as inadequate and recommend that you reject it" or "If the offerer is willing to pay this much for your shares, we all know they must think the company is worth more than that, so don't bite." Target managements had also urged rejection on the basis of highly optimistic projections for future earnings. The Williams Act changed all that. As a target company, we would have to offer the detailed information upon which we based our calculations of the company's worth and our projections of future earnings.

We thus had to make an immediate strategic decision. Should we respond before we were required to do so? An immediate rejection of the tender offer might have a strong psychological impact on shareholders but would also require immediate filing of a 14D Statement together with all our reasons for rejecting the tender, our basis for figuring corporate worth and future earnings, and our evaluation of the inadequacies of the offer. The filing would set in motion a response from Diamond Shamrock and its lawyers, but more important, it would require us to prematurely disclose our contemplated defensive moves.

As the target of an unfriendly tender, we were under no obligation to present our opponents with a detailed evaluation of our company's assets and liabilities. Diamond had made its bid on the basis of published and public information, and we were not required to provide Diamond with any further details until we responded to the offer and filed our 14D Statement. As in war, the best corporate defense often involves control of critical information. In our case, a 14D Statement would give Diamond the most critical information of all: the resources our management had at its command, our estimate of our company's worth, our assessment of our most valuable assets and most troubling liabilities, and the basis for those estimates.

Obviously, if we were to finally conclude that it was in our stockholders' best interest to permit or recommend a sale, we would want to complete the negotiations under the circumstances that would assure the best possible price and conditions. I decided then that we would make no immediate response but wait until we deemed it appropriate or until the ten business days allowed for our response had elapsed. To file public statements before that deadline might limit the price we could ask for the company or otherwise reduce our maneuverability. As far as Diamond's offer was concerned, I considered it to be patently unacceptable, as did my associates. We were strongly tempted to issue a vigorous negative response through the press to our shareholders. But we resisted the temptation—which proved to be one of our better decisions.

· 4 ·

Defining Goals

The team from Jakarta arrived Tuesday morning, May 24. That afternoon we held the first of our daily strategy sessions, involving our staff, our local counsel and New York counsel, and our investment bankers. Given the deadlines, we agreed to reschedule the regular meeting of our Board of Directors, from Wednesday, June 1, to Monday, May 30, the Memorial Day holiday. Since any response by Natomas on the Diamond Shamrock offer would require a Schedule 14D filing to be approved by the Board of Directors, we would need a firm sense of all our options by the thirtieth.

When faced with a takeover threat, corporate managers tend to oppose any suitors. The first response—and it certainly was mine—is to want to fight. If the managers feel that they have done a good job, they resent anyone else coming in and, quite correctly, they sense that they may be fighting for their very jobs. No company needs two chief executive officers or two corporate counsels or two corporate secretaries, to name just a few jeopardized positions. Any takeover inevitably results in the replacement or transfer of many highly compensated and strong-willed executives. The perquisites and prestige of corporate leadership are strong incentives for officers to resist a merger that will abolish their positions. And no one gets very far in business without a highly developed sense of personal competence and a feeling (frequently justified) that no one else can do quite such a good job of running the company. Those feelings, too, are threatened by takeover talk.

In my case, I had assumed the presidency of Natomas, a company with a net book value of $150 million, in 1974. The book value of the company had risen to $1.1 billion by 1983 and the actual value was considerably more. (The book value of a natural resource company is based on the cost of those resources when acquired rather than on the current market value of the reserves.) I felt pride in the job I had done. I also enjoyed my work, my associations, and the place my position afforded me in my community. I had no particular desire to surrender any of it.

Nonetheless, in the cold, harsh light of a takeover threat, if management is to meet its responsibilities it has no choice but to submerge those feelings. Often shareholders, employees, and others dependent on the company will be better off if the takeover is rejected. But sometimes those parties to whom management is responsible will gain more through negotiations with the aggressor, or through acquisition by another company, or even through liquidation of the company in one manner or another. Management must have a clear vision of the alternatives and the will to look as dispassionately as possible at each alternative before deciding what is in the company's best interests.

The general objective of any response to a tender offer seems simple enough: get the best deal. But the best deal for whom? State laws stipulate that corporate directors be held responsible according to the "business judgment rule," which requires them to act (in the language of the courts) "in good faith and in the exercise of honest judgment in the lawful and legitimate furtherance of corporate purposes."*

Auerbach v. *Bennett*, 47 N.Y.2d 619, 629–31, 393 N.E.2d 994, 999–1000, 419 N.Y.S.2d 920, 926–27 (1979).

In a merger or takeover bid, directors, like officers, are faced with some obvious dilemmas, because their own positions are in jeopardy. As a director, one enjoys a certain prestige and entrée into other corporate circles. Each of our twelve outside directors also received an annual retainer of $15,000 and a meeting fee of $800 a day when attending board, committee, shareholder, or advisory meetings. For some of them, retired from their own careers, these directors' fees constituted an important part of their income.

I suppose that it is human nature for the officers and directors of any corporation to see the institution's best interests as coincident with their own. The laws recognize this in holding directors to the business judgment rule. Directors are barred from actions in response to an offer (or even in anticipation of a hostile takeover attempt) if the purpose of those actions is solely their own retention of control. At the same time, the courts have held that perpetuation of control is not presumed to be the directors' motivation simply because their opposition to a tender offer allows them to remain on the board, if they act out of a judgment that this action is in fact in the best interests of the corporation. Of course, any practical application of these decisions entails a certain amount of interpretation. But the courts have tended in recent years to shift the burden of proof toward the shareholder-plaintiffs, who are asked to substantiate claims of bad faith by directors.*

I knew each of our directors personally, liked and respected them all; many had stood with the company through difficult times. I knew that any recommendation on my part that would have the effect of dissolving the company, and with it the Board of Directors, would be difficult. I also

---

* See, for example, *Johnson* v. *Trueblood*, 629 F.2d 287 (3d Cir. 1980), *Cert. denied* 450 U.S. 999 (1981); *Treadway Cos., Inc.* v. *Care Corp.*, 638 F.2d 357 (2d Cir. 1980).

knew that I could count on them to support whatever conclusion seemed in the company's best interests, even at a cost to themselves.

What were the best interests of the corporation? In the simplest terms, Natomas *was* its owners, the holders of its 55.8 million outstanding shares of stock. These shareholders elected the directors, and the directors hired the officers. But nothing in life or business is quite that simple. For example, shareholders rarely fit the stereotype held by the public. There probably never were as many Aunt Maudes with their hundred shares of stock as the public, sometimes encouraged by corporate advertising, assumes. Still, until fairly recently the typical stockholder was an individual who held onto his or her stock for a relatively long period of time, was as interested in dividends and long-term growth as in short-term stock appreciation, and often took a personal interest in the management and day-to-day operation of the company, as I can attest from the sort of questions I have fielded at stockholders' meetings. Precisely for the benefit of these long-term stockholders, measures such as the Williams Act were passed.

In the last few years, this situation has changed dramatically. The principal purchasers of corporate securities have increasingly been pension funds and investor or mutual funds. Many of these funds, competing aggressively for investors' dollars, are run by professional managers whose success is measured by performance, not over several years but from quarter to quarter. This standard of performance discourages fund managers from pondering the long-term health of likely candidates for their portfolios; their attention turns instead to short-term considerations of dividends and appreciation. "Buy low, sell high," always the investors' motto, is now the dominant criterion for fund management, along with "turn a profit now."

The rapid growth of pension and investor funds has created a huge capital base, which has fueled the expansion of American industry by providing necessary resources for new businesses and muscle for the expansion of mature industries. But these large shareholders' needs for short-term performance have also produced a tough new environment for corporate managers. As a friendly investment banker suggested to me, "Stockholder loyalty is measured by an eighth of a point." With short-term performance the primary investment goal, fund managers are likely to sell a stock as soon as they attain a reasonable profit or see a better bargain on the horizon. In addition, fund managers usually do not take much interest in getting to know or understand the management of the companies whose stock they purchase, even though their attitudes and subsequent purchase or sale of the companies' securities have a profound impact on those corporations. Instead, fund managers are likely to size up the management of a public corporation on the basis of short-term performance criteria. Such myopic evaluation is not necessarily to the benefit of either the corporation or, I would submit, society as a whole. This system particularly disadvantages industries that need long-term capital or reseach investments in order to remain innovative and competitive in years ahead.

The psychological impact on management is harder to measure, but its effect is very real. Managers are simply human beings, after all. Even though they are taught, both in business school and in the office, that their first responsibility is to their shareholders, they also respond to the world as they encounter it. What responsibilities can a manager have (or feel) toward a fund, most of whose investors may not even know the names of the companies they hold stock in, and whose portfolio specialists will buy or sell fifty thousand shares on the turn of a few points, with little consideration for the long-range prospects and goals of the company issuing those securities?

This new financial environment also greatly increases the difficulty of protecting a company from a takeover. Since an investment fund frequently stands to make a substantial short-term profit from the premium paid for the target company's stock, the fund is unlikely to resist a tender offer except for the sake of an even better offer. Appeals by the defending management to stockholder loyalty based on the competence and record of the incumbent management rarely impress an investment fund manager bent on a record quarter. Even arguments that point out the weakness of the aggressor company or its management are unlikely to carry much weight. Discussions of future stock values and long-term corporate health are simply not persuasive to stockholders concerned only with short-term profits, "owners" who may not be around long enough to care how the new merger works out.

Thus when management is faced with the threat of a takeover, the question becomes: To which shareholders should one feel responsible? Investors seeking short-term profits will be best served by the highest takeover price, but those who want to see the best long-term results and have the strongest company emerge may be better served by a takeover fight.

The rules that make management equally responsible to all stockholders on a one-share, one-vote basis do not discriminate among these various "owners" of the company, even though their interests may not be identical. The management of a public company also encounters some difficulty simply in knowing who the shareholders are. Large blocks of stock are frequently registered in "street names," names of brokerage houses, or names of foreign banks that conceal the purchasers' true identity.

This problem is further complicated by the very important presence of another constituency—the arbitrageurs. *Arbitrage* is the simultaneous buying and selling of the same commodity or stock in different markets in order to take advantage of price differences, even relatively small ones. For example, if the price of gold is higher on the London market than it is, say, in Zurich, firms with connections in both places may be able to turn a profit by buying gold in Zurich and simultaneously selling it in London.

Arbitrage has probably been around for as long as there have been markets, and students of market behavior credit the practice with bringing a certain stability to prices around the world. In the case of mergers and acquisitions, arbitrage has taken on another meaning as well. Investment banking or brokerage company firms now frequently employ arbitrage specialists who are prepared to buy large positions for their company. If the arbitrageurs sense a takeover may be successful or even that a new bidder will enter the contest at a higher price, they will start buying the stock of the target company. Usually they buy from stockholders who don't have the stomach or patience to wait out a deal or who are unwilling to risk losing the initial market premium in the event the deal falls through.

Arbitrageurs are gutsy players, risking large amounts of capital in return for high potential profits. With a growing number of major players operating on Wall Street, they have become an increasingly significant factor in takeover battles. Their objective is simple: a quick profit, nothing else. They don't buy stock as a long-term investment, and they are not above making threats or bringing lawsuits to coerce a management to move. When the arbitrageurs guess right, they can and do make substantial short-term profits, buying stock on the announcement (or rumor) of a takeover and selling it just as quickly when the deal is consummated or the deal appears to be in trouble. Of course, they also stand to lose money when a takeover does not materialize.

The activity of arbitrageurs frequently accounts for the

heavy volume of trading in a stock between the initial tender offer and the date when the aggressor company can legally begin to purchase the target company's shares. In fact, arbitrageurs figure predominantly in the aggressor's offensive strategy. The premium offered by the aggressor—the difference between the current market price and the tender offer price—is partially designed to draw arbitrageurs and their great purchasing power into the market and to shift the stock from individual stockholders, who might have some attachment to management, to the arbitrageurs, whose only business is to sell the stock quickly to the highest bidder.

We had to assume that the arbitrageurs had played a role in the heavy fluctuations in the price of Natomas stock over the last several months, whenever takeover rumors had surfaced. We also assumed, although we could not prove it, that the heavy trading in Natomas stock during the week before the actual tender was partially due to arbitrageur activity.

When arbitrageurs take a sizable position in a company's stock, their action can have a self-fulfilling quality and will clearly affect the outcome of a takeover battle. Not only do they vote their shares for whichever side figures to permit them the maximum profit, but they can exert other pressures as well. For example, if they believe the transaction is likely to be consummated, they may arbitrage between the stock of the two companies. In the case of Natomas and Diamond Shamrock, I am sure that the arbitrageurs were simultaneously selling the latter and buying the former based on the proposed exchange ratio, as long as there was a sufficient spread between the two stocks. We later estimated that as much as 40 percent of Natomas's shares were in the hands of arbitrageurs by the time we completed negotiations with Diamond Shamrock. And part of the litigation over our preferred shares (a story I'll get to a little later) was undoubtedly due to the action of arbitrageurs who had guessed wrong about the effect of the merger on our preferred securities.

Our first priority, to get the best deal for our stockholders, proved, then, to be more complicated than it originally appeared. Again, the feelings of management toward the variously motivated stockholders should in theory be irrelevant. However, it certainly affects a manager's thinking when he or she knows that a significant percentage of the company's stock is probably held by traders who are, in effect, betting against the company, counting on its failure to defend against the aggressor.

Too, I have long felt that management's responsibility to others, especially employees, is not a great deal less than that to stockholders. Even the courts have held that the duty of directors and management extends beyond shareholders to employees, customers, the local community, and the general public.* Natomas had more than 5,350 employees, many of whom had been with the company for years, had stayed with us during difficult times and contributed to our growth when we had prospered. I was determined that their welfare not be forgotten when we considered the options facing us. Our other responsibilities were more abstract, but nevertheless important. As a company

---

* See *Herald Co.* v. *Seawell*, 472 F.2d 1081 (10th Cir. 1972) (employee morale, local community, public interest); *Abramson* v. *Nytronics, Inc.*, 312 F. Supp. 519, 531 (S.D.N.Y. 1970) (employee morale); *Boyertown Burial Casket Co.* v. *Amedco, Inc.*, 407 F. Supp. 811, 814, 817 (E.D. Pa. 1976) (employee morale, public interest); *Universal Leaf Tobacco* v. *Congoleum Corp.*, 554 F.2d 1283, 1284 (4th Cir. 1977) (customers); *Elco Corp.* v. *Microdot Inc.*, 360 F. Supp. 741, 753–54 (D. Del. 1973) (customers, public); cf. *Missouri Portland Cement Co.* v. *Cargill, Inc.*, 498 F.2d 851, 869–70 (2d Cir.), *cert. denied*, 419 U.S. 883 (1974) (importance of employee morale discounted, but public interest considered). See generally Lipton, *Takeover Bids in the Target's Boardroom*, 35 Bus. Law. 101, 102 & n.7 (1979).

largely involved in energy, we had, I felt, a responsibility to see that the nonrenewable assets that we managed were used as well and carefully as possible. I could not guarantee that a new owner would bring the same concern, and I wanted to do what I could to see those resources remain with us or pass into hands that would care for them. In addition, Natomas had played a significant role in the economic and cultural life of the San Francisco Bay Area, as a major taxpayer, through the compounding effect of our multimillion-dollar annual payroll, and through the million dollars or more we donated each year to charitable and cultural causes. I wanted to make every effort to minimize any detrimental effects a change in Natomas would have on these community responsibilities.

We had a variety of complex goals, then, summed up by that deceptively simple phrase, "getting the best deal for the company." We knew that Diamond Shamrock had offered $23 in cash for 51 percent of our shares, which had been selling not long before for $13 to $15. We had to find a way to top that offer, to block it, or to give stockholders a sound reason for not tendering their shares. Otherwise all our other goals would become irrelevant as the arbitrageurs and other stockholders, given a chance to receive a 50 percent premium for at least half their shares, succumbed to Diamond Shamrock's entreaties. And there wasn't much time.

· 5 ·

Assessing Strategies

As Tuesday dawned we accelerated our pace and grouped our tasks into four major areas.

Diamond Shamrock had offered to purchase for $23 per share up to 30,400,000 shares, which, combined with the 170,300 shares they already held, would give them voting control of the company. We didn't know how much higher they were willing to go. The cash offered came to nearly $700 million. In addition, their cost would be increased by standby costs paid to maintain the commitments for that money up to the date the acquisition was completed. For the other 49 percent of our shares Diamond had announced that it "intended" to offer 0.92 of a share of Diamond stock for each. But that offer clearly was not firm. With the advent of the tender offer Diamond Shamrock stock had slipped by Tuesday from $25.50 a share (at which 0.92 of a share equaled $23.46) to $24. If the deal was badly perceived, Diamond stock could fall even farther, resulting in considerable uncertainty for our shareholders.

We sketched out four areas on which to concentrate our attention: (1) evaluating the tender offer, its short-term and long-term benefits for stockholders and others to whom we felt responsible; (2) assessing the possibility of devising better alternatives within the operating time constraints;

(3) developing tactics to induce Diamond Shamrock to improve its offer; and (4) seeking ways to block the deal if it did not seem in the stockholders' best interests, or to delay the transaction in order to give ourselves more time to develop alternatives.

Those tasks, of course, overlapped extensively. Evaluation of Diamond Shamrock's offer fell first to our in-house financial and operating staff, as well as to our investment bankers and to our outside legal counsel. The holders of the 51 percent of the shares Diamond Shamrock was offering to buy would have their cash. The value to them was simple enough: $23 a share for each share tendered and bought. For the owners of the remaining 49 percent of the shares, however, the outcome was not that clear. (And if more than the 30 million shares Diamond had agreed to purchase were tendered and Diamond only accepted a pro-rated number of shares from each shareholder, then all our shareholders would have some stock subject to later disposition.) Although Diamond had indicated an "intention" to exchange Diamond shares for the remaining shares of Natomas, they were under no obligation to do so. Some of the shareholders could find themselves holding a minority interest in a subsidiary of Diamond Shamrock, a position that might leave them with little political leverage and limited marketability for their shares.

In addition, how strong a company would the new Diamond Shamrock be? What would be the impact on future profits of its borrowing $700 million (or more, if we negotiated a higher cash deal) to complete the transaction? Could we anticipate other problems with the new company that would prompt us to oppose the offer or to urge our shareholders to resist? Within hours our staff and the investment bankers and legal counsel would produce preliminary answers.

Second, we needed to examine all possible alternatives,

proposals we could either offer directly to our shareholders or use as leverage in negotiating a better deal from Diamond Shamrock. Some of the possibilities included—in the colorful language of acquisition and merger warfare— finding a white knight (another company willing to make a better offer than Diamond Shamrock), or employing the recently popularized Pac-Man defense, in which we, as the target company, would make a counter–tender offer for Diamond Shamrock's shares. Other alternatives, in theory, included creating a special issue of preferred stock that would carry special voting rights and selling those shares to a friendly third party who would oppose the takeover. Or we could borrow or sell assets and use the proceeds to buy back our own shares at a higher, and what we believed more realistic, price than that offered by Diamond. Most of these alternatives required significant amounts of cash and credit, far more than Natomas had on hand at the time. Charlie Lee began the task of lining up the necessary bank credit. Our goal was a minimum of a billion dollars. Other members of our staff as well as the investment bankers pursued a number of variations on each of the possibilities.

Of course, any choice of a defensive strategy depended on our conclusions as to what Natomas as a whole, as well as each of its parts, was really worth. Fortunately, our corporate development group had designed sophisticated computer models of each of the major segments of the company, partly in anticipation of such a need but principally as a tool for making capital investment decisions. Those models and the expertise to manipulate them were suddenly worth millions of dollars. By varying the assumptions— such as future energy prices, rates of inflation, interest costs, or estimated production rates—the models, within hours, produced ranges of values, division by division. It was a task that once might have required long weeks to accomplish, or more likely would never have been undertaken. But we knew our computer models could give us the information we needed—and in takeover negotiations, information translates into power.

Our third task was to pressure Diamond Shamrock to sweeten its offer, in the eventuality that we wound up making a deal with them. The best way to prompt a new Diamond offer, of course, was to locate a better alternative, a third party who would engage Diamond in a bidding war. But there were other, more subtle, tactics to employ as well. As I mentioned earlier, we had decided to tell Diamond Shamrock absolutely no more than necessary about our response. When Diamond's chairman, William Bricker, called me on Monday, May 23, and suggested that we get together as soon as possible to conduct friendly negotiations, I was tempted to reject his offer out of hand, adding that there were friendlier ways to begin negotiations than with an unsolicited tender offer. But I simply demurred: "I have not seen your letter yet; when I do you will hear from us in due course." I advised my associates that this would be our stance. We would delay any discussions with Diamond Shamrock until we deemed it in our best interests to meet.

We knew that any specific Natomas response would require us to file a Schedule 14D Statement, information that would immediately become public. But we had no intention of putting into Diamond Shamrock's hands anything that might be used against us or that would divulge our strategy and offer them the opportunity to respond. We wanted to keep Diamond Shamrock in the dark as long as possible, giving them no grounds to assume that we were anxious or panicky.

For precisely the same reasons, we declined to discuss our strategies with the press, although we did nothing (through a stream of "No comment" responses) to discourage or correct speculations that we were talking with others and developing other options. Similarly, we scrupulously avoided confirming or denying our not too well hidden campaign to increase our lines of credit. Word circulates rather freely in financial circles, and Diamond Shamrock, without knowing the exact extent of our credit lines, couldn't help hearing that we were successful in our efforts. All these moves were calculated to communicate loudly, if vaguely, that we were exploring an array of options. We kept our eyes open for any signs of how anxious Diamond Shamrock might be to make a deal.

Fourth, our lawyers plunged aggressively into the task of finding ways to block or slow the timetable. We knew that devising an alternative deal might take weeks or months. But Diamond Shamrock would be free to purchase shares once the waiting period expired on June 20 unless we could find a legitimate delaying action. Delay, we felt, could conceivably bring a better offer from Dallas. So we set ourselves to identifying potential grounds for stopping the clock.

We briefly considered a set of tactics known as "shark repellent" measures, acts whose main purpose is to make a takeover less likely or at least more difficult. Many variations on this theme have been developed over the years by threatened corporations. Several involve corporate charter amendments, such as requiring that a takeover must be approved by a vote of up to 80 percent of the outstanding shares of the company. Another provides staggered terms for members of the Board of Directors—typically that only one-third of the directors come up for election each year— to make it more difficult for a minority to control or even gain a seat on the board. When a tender is made for a majority or all of the company's shares, however, these measures cannot prevent a takeover but only delay it or make the company less attractive as a target. But in our case, they made no sense. Any corporate amendment would take weeks to put in place and would require shareholder approval. The time to put shark repellent provisions in effect is before a tender offer has been made, not after the battle has begun. Under the circumstances, such measures did not warrant any expenditure of our time or attention.

Other alternatives at least held out more potential. We could make an acquisition in exchange for Natomas stock in order to dilute the position of Diamond or to make it more costly for them to gain control. Or we could place a block of stock in friendly hands, though sometimes these "friends" prove to be less than friendly later on. We could sell shares of a "blocking" preferred stock with special voting privileges, issued to an ally who would be expected to vote those shares in opposition to the takeover. Or we could make a defensive acquisition, that is, purchase a company or assets for cash in order to either increase Natomas's debt and thereby make us less attractive, or create antitrust problems for Diamond. The courts have ruled that such maneuvers can be judged illegal if their "sole purpose" is to thwart a tender offer, but they have been less decisive in their rulings on such purchases shown to have been made primarily, but not solely, for defensive purposes.*

The strategy of adopting a so-called poison pill had not yet been developed at the time of our battle, but would subsequently be initially employed by Household International. Their plan involved issuing warrants to shareholders that in the event of a hostile takeover could be exercised to buy shares of the acquiring company at half the market value. Designed to scare off potential acquirers, the poison pill is no doubt going to be the subject of substantial litigation.

* See, for example, *Anaconda Co.* v. *Crane Co.*, 411 F.Supp. 1210, 1219–20 (S.D.N.Y. 1975); *Panter* v. *Marshall Field & Co.*, 486 F.Supp. 1168 (N.D. Ill. 1980), *Aff'd* 646 F.2d 271 (7th Cir. 1981), *Cert. denied* 102 S.Ct. 658 (1981).

Another approach, and one we took seriously, was to seek to block Diamond Shamrock from purchasing shares of Natomas through a preliminary injunction, on the grounds of inadequate disclosure. At the time of the tender offer Diamond Shamrock was required in its initial filing with the SEC to disclose any material information relevant to the proposed purchase and the effect of that purchase on the parent company. In addition, Diamond had routinely made periodic required filings with the New York Stock Exchange and with the SEC. Our local counsel, Morrison and Foerster, began a methodical scrutiny of each of those filings.

They also began an extensive search for anything else that might be grounds for preventive litigation. One promising legal area concerned our ownership of American President Lines (APL). As a subsidized United States flag carrier, APL was under the jurisdiction of the Federal Maritime Commission, which had the final authority to approve or disapprove a change of ownership of the company. In addition, we held oil exploration and production contracts with the Indonesian government. A change of ownership might require formal approval or at least acquiescence by that government. We did not know if any of these issues were sufficient grounds for an injunction, but we intended to explore all of them.

Now, too, our legal and public relations personnel and consultants began outlining a case that we could take directly to our shareholders. We had little reason to believe that many shareholders (especially those who were only along for the quick profit) would respond to appeals to their loyalty, but we did believe that we could pique considerable interest if we could demonstrate that shares in Natomas were worth considerably more than $23, or that shareholders who did not tender at that price would be at economic or legal risk if the deal were completed.

For all we knew, we might be grasping at straws, but at least we had handfuls of them. The task groups, with both precise and broad mandates, were instructed to report each morning for the rest of the week, and more often if there were significant developments.

· 6 ·

Natomas

This seems a good point to speak briefly about the history of Natomas, my association with the company, why Natomas was vulnerable to a takeover attempt, and what we knew about our company's strengths and weaknesses as we sought to maneuver for the best possible response to the Diamond Shamrock tender offer.

I had been in the energy business for most of my working life, first as an accountant and then as an operating executive with Douglas Oil Company, a small West Coast refining company later acquired by Continental Oil Company. In 1964 I met Dr. Armand Hammer of Occidental Petroleum and joined that company as chief financial officer. In my eight years with Occidental, during its formative years, I learned a great deal about acquisitions and mergers. The year before I joined the company, Occidental had had sales of about $30 million; when I left in 1972 sales exceeded $3 billion. I claim no credit for that growth: it was the work of Occidental's acquisitive genius Dr. Hammer, but it was a remarkable training ground. In my own area of responsibility, bank credit had grown from a few million dollars to over $600 million in 1972, as acquisition followed upon acquisition. For two years after leaving Occidental in August 1972, I worked independently as a consultant in the field of corporate finance. In June 1973 I was introduced to Natomas Company.

Chandler Ide, then president and chief executive officer of Natomas, had indicated that he wished to retire the following year when he reached sixty-five. I had decided that I wanted either to continue consulting, which I enjoyed, or to run a company. It was obvious that Natomas had problems, and it had not made a lot of money in recent years. And I was reluctant to move to San Francisco from Southern California, where we had lived for thirty years and had deep roots in the community. But the prospect was intriguing. Chandler Ide was a delightful person to work with and, perhaps more importantly, the world of petroleum was changing dramatically. In October 1973 I accepted a seat on the Board of Directors of Natomas. By December the price of oil had tripled (although I wouldn't want to claim a cause-and-effect relationship between those events). In April 1974 I became president and CEO of the company.

The origins of Natomas dated back to the Natomas Water Company, founded in 1851 to supply water to gold rush mining camps, and later engaged in gold dredging, principally along the American River in the Sacramento Valley of California. Modern-day Natomas was incorporated in the Sacramento Valley in 1928 and moved to San Francisco in 1961.

The "modern" Natomas was the creation of Ralph K. Davies, a canny San Francisco entrepreneur who died in 1971. Davies (whom I never met) had been elected as the youngest director of Standard Oil Company of California before World War II, and had gone on to serve as the nation's petroleum administrator during the war. After the war Davies and his associates, among other accomplishments, acquired the controlling interest in American President Lines (APL) and negotiated a merger of that interest into Natomas, then a somewhat moribund company listed on the New York Stock Exchange. Davies emerged as the principal shareholder and chief executive officer of the company. An international oil man by training and instinct, he also negotiated the acquisition of Iapco (Indonesian American Petroleum Company), which later became the basis of Natomas's highly successful Indonesian oil operations.

By 1974 the company's net book value was stated as approximately $150 million. Of that, about $65 million represented a 54 percent ownership of APL, which, based on its recent earnings, was a value hard to justify. The balance of Natomas's assets consisted of interests in two petroleum exploration and production contracts in Indonesia and some miscellaneous assets: a refinery in Antigua that had lost money since its inception, a gasoline marketing operation in Quebec, and real estate holdings, mostly in gold-dredging waste land near Sacramento. Needless to say, the company was a strange hybrid, a character it never fully escaped during my tenure, and one of the reasons that analysts continued to have trouble assessing its real value.

When I became CEO, I had serious doubts about the shipping end of the company and assumed that we would dispose of it when we had a chance. My first priority, however, was to exploit the rising price of crude oil by attending to our Indonesian contracts. When I made my preliminary analysis of the company, in mid 1973, Indonesian crude oil was selling at about $3.65 a barrel and, compared with lower-cost Saudi Arabian oil, it was expensive to produce. Natomas's Indonesian contracts were all offshore in the Java Sea and required facilities far more costly than onshore operations. In addition, our Indonesian oil was produced from geologically complex structures and smaller fields than those on shore in the Middle East. At the same time, Indonesia had a highly productive work force, a favorable environment in which to operate, a stable and progressive government, and clear proximity to Pacific Basin markets. The crude oil itself was generally low in sulfur and of high quality. At the right price it could be profitable. After my preliminary analysis in 1973, I reviewed the economics of the operation with Chandler Ide. "There is no way that operation can really make any money without a significant increase in the price of crude oil," I said. "The price would have to go up at least a dollar a barrel." By December 1973 the Yom Kippur War and the sudden panic-motivated shortages had driven Indonesian crude oil up nearly $7 a barrel, to above $10 a barrel. By May, when I became president, Indonesian crude was at $13 a barrel. We now had the chance to make some real money—if we handled it right.

Natomas operated in Indonesia under production sharing contracts with Pertamina, Indonesia's national petroleum company. A thirty-year agreement signed in 1968 gave Natomas a 53 percent interest in the Southeast Sumatra contract area, with Natomas also to serve as operator. Another thirty-year agreement completed in 1967 in the Northwest Java contract area gave Natomas 34 percent of the contractors' interest, with Atlantic Richfield Company (Arco) as operator.

Over the next nine years the Indonesian operations became a remarkable success, one attributable, I feel, to two main factors. First, we maintained an excellent, if somewhat stormy, relationship with the Indonesian government. Our "firm" thirty-year petroleum exploration and production contracts had been renegotiated three times, at the request and obviously to the advantage of Indonesia; Natomas approached these negotiations with an attitude as cooperative and constructive as possible. We further strengthened relations in 1982 by naming Edward E. Masters, a former U.S. ambassador to Indonesia, as our senior vice-president for international affairs. I took considerable personal pride in our success and one of my major concerns, from the moment we knew of the Diamond Shamrock tender offer, was whether Diamond, with no experience in Indonesia, would be able to continue to maintain and improve that relationship.

The other factor that contributed to our success in the 1970s was our ability to develop our discoveries in record time. We organized an aggressive exploration program, and both the competence and the morale of our local Indonesian and expatriate staffs were high. In addition, our field managers standardized production facilities, accelerated training of Indonesian technical and mechanical staff, and developed a variety of innovative techniques—all of which gave Natomas one of the fastest start-up schedules in the industry. On the average we needed only six months from the time a field was confirmed until the start of production. Would this be maintained under new ownership? Only time would tell.

By the end of 1982, the gross remaining proven developed oil reserves in both our contract areas were estimated to be nearly 400 million barrels. The potential reserves, particularly in the area operated by Arco, was several times that amount. Even with the continued softening of worldwide oil prices throughout 1982, the Indonesian contracts represented a substantial asset. During the preceding two years the contracts had produced $271 million in operating income for Natomas. They had to be one of the prime attractions for a potential buyer.

Our other hydrocarbon energy operations, however, had not fared so well. Our North American petroleum operations lost $66.6 million in 1982, after a net operating profit of $20.4 million in 1981. The 1982 decline resulted from a $75 million write-down of the value of Natomas's U.S. petroleum-producing assets, along with higher operating expenses and reduced demand for natural gas. Our Canadian petroleum marketing operations registered a small operating profit in 1982, but our coal operations lost money due primarily to weak market conditions. Our computer models indicated we would be lucky to get $300 million for all these segments combined. We sensed that domestic oil and gas, as well as coal, were in for even tougher sledding. (At this writing, in early 1985, prices for all three commodities are still falling.)

The crown jewel of our energy assets, outside of Indonesia, however, was our 50 percent interest in the Geysers Geothermal field in Northern California, a joint venture with Union Oil Company, the operator.

The geothermal joint venture had been my first energy diversification move at Natomas and one of which I felt justifiably proud. We acquired our interest in two stages, the first in 1974 when we outbid several competitors with an offer of $40 million for a 25 percent interest then held by Thermal Power Company. In 1982 we acquired another 25 percent through a $400 million bid for Magma Power Company, an acquisition that was not contested by any other company, but had initially been "unfriendly" as far as Magma management was concerned. The exponential difference in price between the two acquisitions, incidentally, reflected the escalation of energy prices between 1974 and 1982. In going after Magma, we had concluded that the uniqueness of the Geysers resource base assured that someone would move to acquire the company—and soon. Our preemptive bid proved successful.

The Geysers is the largest commercial geothermal electricity-generating operation in the world; with fifteen generating plants it is estimated to be only about half developed. The operation produces cost-efficient and economical "dry" steam that flows directly through the local utility's electricity-generating turbines. Compared with fossil fuels or nuclear energy, the Geysers' geothermal generation is clean, safe, and substantially less expensive.

Natomas held a contract with Pacific Gas and Electric Company (PG&E) that pledged the utility to buy steam supplied by the Geysers project for fifty years after the last geothermal generating plant became operational—a start-up expected during the 1990s. The price for steam under the contract is based on a formula indexed to the cost of fossil and nuclear fuels used by PG&E's other generating plants. Between 1974 and 1982 the annual price PG&E paid for steam increased from 3.8 mils per kilowatt hour to over 35 mils, and we expected it to increase again in 1983. Natomas's operating income from our share of geothermal operations showed a parallel increase, from $3.0 million in 1974, to $27.9 million in 1981, to $31.4 million in 1982, even though PG&E used less geothermal capacity in 1982 because the previous winter's heavy rainfall increased the availability of hydroelectric power.

With new drilling and new plants, Natomas's share of steam reserves at the Geysers at the end of 1982, measured on a thermal-unit equivalent, was 144 million barrels of oil. We had paid $40 million for the 25 percent interest we acquired in 1974, and $400 million for another 25 percent interest in 1981. By 1983, I was convinced that Natomas's share of the Geysers was or would soon be worth $1 billion, an estimate we could support with our computer projections. I was not sure, however, that we could find a buyer at that figure in the very short time now facing us.

Another major accomplishment at Natomas had been our success in turning around American President Lines (APL). By 1983 I considered it to be one of the company's major assets.

APL was an old and famous company, originally called the Dollar Steamship Lines. Along the way it had acquired the even-older Pacific Mail Steamship Company, founded in the 1849 gold rush days, when the company's ships made runs from the East Coast to San Francisco via Cape Horn.

Pacific Mail Steamship was the first U.S. company to establish regular steamship service to Japan and China, and offered round-the-world service as early as 1925. The APL fleet was requisitioned for active Navy and Army service during World War II, after which it was returned to private ownership. Subsequently, APL also acquired the American Mail Line, another West Coast–based shipping company. APL had been making substantial efforts during the years to keep pace with changes in the industry. By 1973 it had almost completed converting its fleet to freight containerization and had eliminated the last of its unprofitable passenger lines.

When I came aboard in 1974, APL earnings had declined from an average of slightly over $7.5 million in the last half of the 1960s to about $1.1 million in the first four years of the 1970s, including a $10 million loss in 1973. Natomas owned about 54 percent of the business, with the majority of the remainder owned by The Signal Companies. Although annual profits in the preceding ten years had averaged $7.3 million, in the mid 1970s profits were declining, even though the company received yearly government subsidies of $35 million to $50 million. (Through the Maritime Administration, the federal government provides subsidies to partially compensate shipping companies, which are heavily regulated, for the relatively greater expense, largely wages, of vessel operation under United States registry.) When I joined Natomas I was unacquainted with the transportation business, but I could see that Natomas was putting a lot of effort into a company whose earnings were declining, and I was less than enthusiastic about maintaining that segment of the business.

My first response was to announce that Natomas's interest in APL was for sale. I approached Signal, but they indicated no interest in buying our share. Instead, they said they would be happy to sell their share if we could find a buyer for the whole company. So I made the "for sale" notices more prominent, but still no one broke down our door to acquire the company. The absence of any prospective buyers wasn't really surprising; at the time APL wasn't much of a bargain.

APL had failed to do some important long-term planning. For example, most APL shore facilities were located on either public ports, where the company had to share space with a variety of shipping lines, or on short-term leases subject to cancellation or escalation in cost. The company had converted from bulk-type operations to containerized freight operations—a costly process yet certainly a move in the right direction—but most of their new containers and other equipment were leased, a decision that once probably seemed wise but now was needlessly costly. Finally, APL's internal organization was weak. All in all, the company was not in a strong competitive position.

During my first two years with Natomas, while I concentrated on the energy side of the company, I tried to ignore APL or sell it, but to no avail. I finally concluded that I could no longer avoid the shipping business: it wouldn't go away, and I couldn't find anyone to take it off our hands. We had to make a strategic move. I called in our corporate development staff and ordered a study of the entire liner industry, not just APL. In order to decide what to do with the company we would need to understand containerized freight shipping, its future, and how APL stood in relation to its competitors. We interviewed a number of consultants and engaged the Boston firm of Temple, Barker and Sloane, who appeared to have outstanding knowledge and expertise in the field.

My instructions to our staff and the consultants were simple: "Consider every alternative. No option, including liquidation of the company, is unacceptable." In fact, my guess was that liquidation was probably our best move.

The study extended over a full year, from 1976 to 1977. At the time the top management of APL failed to take the study seriously. The then-president told one of his associates, "Hell, when this study is done nothing will come of it." He was wrong; the exercise proved most successful. In the simplest terms we found that APL was well positioned, with good equipment, reasonably good port facilities, and an excellent reputation, especially in the Far East, throughout its hundred-year history. True, it was making money on only a few of its routes, while losing almost as much on others; its management was weak and morale low. But with some quick fundamental changes (such as terminating the money-losing round-the-world service) and a reasonable injection of capital, it appeared that APL could make money.

This certainly was not the conclusion I or the consultants had anticipated when we began the study, but the documentation was thorough and I was willing to accept the results. The implementation phase began with a search for someone to run the company. Frankly, the shipping industry at that time was not awash in talent. The industry had not been profitable, its managers had been poorly compensated, and good management people had not gravitated to it. Within the past three decades the United States shipping industry had shrunk to a relatively insignificant position in relation to the nation's industry as a whole. For example, if in 1977 all the U.S. flag ocean-liner companies had merged together, the resulting company would have been smaller than a medium-sized oil company.

Our initial search for a new president proved discouraging, and I reluctantly concluded that there was no one in the shipping industry whom I wanted to hire. So I turned to my staff at Natomas and asked Bruce Seaton, then a senior vice-president of Natomas who had served on the APL Board of Directors, to take the position on a temporary basis.

At first Bruce was understandably quite reluctant. One of the harshest critics of the APL operation, he advocated our disposing of it. He wanted assurances that if he were to accept the job he could come back to the energy side of the business as quickly as possible. My response: "When you find somebody else to run APL, we'll talk about that." It was a real challenge and Bruce performed well. With the blueprint developed from our study and the help of our consultants, he turned the company around. In one year it became a significantly profitable operation, in part a result of Bruce's success in attracting talented young people, many from our competitors, into the company.

At that time Natomas owned 54 percent of APL, which existed as a separate organization. Once it became clear that we had a profitable company I concluded that we ought to acquire the minority interests. In addition to tax benefits to the consolidated company, we would gain complete flexibility in running the company. After negotiating a trade for Signal's 45 percent interest in APL for 12.5 percent of Natomas stock, we merged out the balance of the minority shareholders. APL became a wholly owned subsidiary of Natomas.

Along the way we made some important operating decisions. The Atlantic Straits service was terminated in 1976, and the round-the-world service in 1977. The vessels from those two operations were redeployed in the Pacific Basin, where we were convinced that the prospects for real economic growth were strong. We inaugurated a $600 million capital program designed to upgrade our fleet, equipment, and shoreside facilities. We ordered three new C-9s, the largest (860 feet long) and most advanced container ships ever built in the U.S., and we improved the inland transportation part of our business by negotiating new and less expensive arrangements with the U.S. railroads, purchasing our own railcars and running our own trains from coast to coast. In addition, APL pioneered a network of rail connections that allowed the company's Linertrains, which carried APL cargo exclusively, to bypass the stops conventional trains made to break up and reassemble cars in railyards all over the country. (This effort still continues, incidentally. In 1983 the company completed research and development of a lightweight railcar capable of carrying four containers, two containers stacked on top of two others, at a marginal increase in railroad locomotive power and no increase in train crew.)

In 1980, at the beginning of a rate war, Seaton deliberately cut the company's operations to reduce costs and to concentrate on high-value traffic, such as refrigerated products, electronics, and designer clothing. That decision cost APL some market position in the short-term but increased its profits.

The rejuvenation of APL was a major accomplishment. Earnings had averaged $7.3 million a year in the decade preceding our restructuring; they soared to a record $59.2 million in 1979 and continued to hit $40 million to $50 million until 1983. Then a series of factors—a worldwide business slump, rising interest rates, the initial cost of introducing three new ships and equipment, and declining exports occasioned by an overpriced dollar—converged to produce a first-quarter loss of $19.7 million. This turnabout contributed to Natomas's overall vulnerability in the spring of 1983, even though APL had begun to rebound by the time of the tender offer, finishing the year with a $25 million profit.

In addition to its energy and transportation divisions, Natomas also had a small real estate company that was developing and marketing homes and commercial sites in two model communities near Sacramento, on the land inherited from the company's gold-dredging days. The other prime asset of the real estate company, the twenty-two–story International Building in San Francisco, in which Natomas's headquarters were located, had been sold in April, prior to the Diamond Shamrock tender offer, for $53.5 million.

Although I was confident of Natomas's long-term prospects at the time of the tender offer, I also knew that the company was vulnerable to a takeover bid. Not only were the courts and regulatory agencies allowing mergers and acquisitions of giant companies, without great concern for antitrust implications (witness the demise of Conoco, Marathon, Cities Service, and Getty, topped later by the purchase of Gulf by Standard of California), but declining oil prices made energy companies attractive objects for acquisition. The prevailing oil glut, which had driven oil prices down, had weakened the market price of oil company stocks, including Natomas. In the long run, mainland U.S. oil and gas reserves were being depleted more rapidly than they were being replaced, but temporarily it was less expensive to acquire reserves by buying up a producing company rather than finding and developing new reserves.

Natomas stock had suffered for some time for other reasons as well. As recently as 1980, the stock hit a peak of $45 a share, only to fall back to the $15 to $16 range in which it was languishing before the tender offer. Most of that slippage followed the general collapse of oil prices, but our stock's decline was compounded by the losses (even though I saw them as temporary) sustained by other sectors of the company, including APL. Natomas as a whole lost $6.6 million in the first quarter of 1983. In order to conserve cash, we sold the office building and in January lowered the quarterly dividend from 35 cents to 20 cents a share. I also reduced our work force by 6 percent and announced that the top five corporate officers, including myself, would take 10 percent pay cuts for the year.

These setbacks were real, but I still felt that Natomas stock had long been undervalued, selling at a relatively low price-earnings multiple. (A stock's *price-earnings multiple* is the ratio of the trading price of a share to the earnings per share for the preceding twelve months.) Natomas frequently traded at as low as three or four times earnings, compared with the seven to eight times earnings typical of domestic oil companies. This low price multiple was an invitation for a takeover, even though it represented traders' perceptions more than the real condition of the company. Natomas's earnings were considered somewhat suspect because of the company's concentration in Indonesia. Oil analysts, who advise the major investors, viewed the Indonesian contracts as politically risky, even though Indonesia had been unusually stable in its relationship to the oil companies, certainly compared with the Middle East. Among the factors that contributed to this stability was Indonesia's dependence on its petroleum exports for badly needed foreign exchange. The fifth most populous nation in the world, Indonesia, though a poor country measured by per capita income, is rich in natural resources and maintained an average growth rate of 5.3 percent (gross national product) between 1970 and 1978. In addition, because oil fields in off-shore Indonesia (in our case in the Java Sea) tend to be small by Middle Eastern standards and frequently more difficult to produce, the Indonesians were compelled to rely heavily on the seasoned expertise of the foreign producing companies. But all these factors were seldom given much weight by the analysts.

Even more confusing to oil analysts was Natomas's ownership of APL, which competed in an industry the oil people neither understood nor tried to understand. Because there was no company listed on the New York Stock Exchange whose primary business was in the United States ocean-liner trade, there were no analysts who specialized in the field, and no one on Wall Street understood it well. (The largest ocean-liner companies were Sealand, an R. J. Reynolds subsidiary, APL, and the privately owned U.S. Lines.)

That APL was operated independently of the Natomas Energy Company, did not rely on its parent company for underwriting its debt or operations, and consistently paid up dividends to the parent—all failed to impress. In the eyes of the investment community, Natomas vaguely resembled that out-of-favor phenomenon, the conglomerate, or at best an oil company with a strange, unpredictable appendage. Despite APL's several years of excellent earnings, its loss in the first quarter of 1983 led analysts to describe the company in such terms as Natomas's "troubled shipping holdings" or "ailing business in ocean shipping." Yet other analysts treated APL as if it were invisible; one, quoted in a Reuters story, simply said that Natomas had "a golden goose," but that "all its eggs are in one basket," meaning the Indonesian oil contracts.

At Natomas, we were comfortable with the APL relationship, which had been very important to our profits when oil prices had started to drop. But despite a long-term public relations program addressed to the financial community, our stock continued to languish. And in May 1983, when Diamond made its move, we had just reported the large APL loss for the first quarter of the year and a small loss for the entire company.

So we knew we were likely to have difficulty, particularly in the few weeks we had to maneuver, to realize the full value of the company from either Diamond Shamrock or an alternative bidder. We had to admit grudgingly that Diamond Shamrock had timed its offer quite skillfully. Now it was up to us to make the best of it.

· 7 ·

Diamond

Tom Neville had his first report on Diamond Shamrock on my desk Monday morning. We continued through the week to add particulars to our picture of Diamond, as our researchers waded through the vast amount of information available on the public company. We had, of course, Diamond's tender offer and the accompanying SEC filings. But we also had access to the schedules Diamond had filed with recent stock offerings, their annual reports filed with the New York Stock Exchange, and the analyses (with allowances for exaggeration) prepared by brokers and research firms for clients considering the purchase of Diamond stock. Diamond Shamrock, or course, had made use of similar information about Natomas in setting its bid price and preparing its strategy.

We learned of Diamond's initial intentions regarding APL through filings with the Maritime Administration. And we monitored the ever-present rumors emanating from the financial community. We could not read the minds of Diamond's management, and no one there was any more likely than we were to divulge points of strategy. But we had to try to piece together a sufficiently clear picture to plan our moves.

Some questions about Diamond were critical: Why were

they interested in Natomas? What did they hope to accomplish through a merger? How badly did they want to complete a deal? Any counteroffer we might make would depend in part on how accurately we assessed the answers to those key questions.

In addition, we were looking for flaws, any flaws, in Diamond's offer, its filings, or its operations that might constitute legal or other grounds for slowing down or halting the tender offer. Finally, we wanted to know what kind of company we were dealing with. If we were to consider recommending a merger to our shareholders (either on Diamond's terms or through a newly negotiated agreement), we needed to be able to say, honestly, that association with Diamond Shamrock, on the terms set by the final proposal, would be in the best interest of our stockholders and would constitute the best feasible alternative. I saw little likelihood that their original proposal would meet our criteria. Even if the cash paid for the 51 percent of Natomas shares was reasonable, which we did not believe was the case, there was considerable doubt about the value of the paper our shareholders would receive for the remaining 49 percent of their stock. We couldn't even be sure that the subsequent merger would take place at all.

If Natomas was perceived (inaccurately in our view) as an energy company with peripheral holdings in transportation, then it appeared to us that Diamond Shamrock was trying to shed its image as a chemical company which dabbled in energy. Diamond, whose motto is "the resourceful company," was the result of a 1967 merger between Diamond Alkali Company of Cleveland and the Shamrock Oil and Gas Company. Diamond described itself in a 1983 prospectus as "a domestic integrated oil and gas company with interests in coal and chemicals." As recently as 1975, however, a variety of chemical interests (industrial chemicals, plastics and resins, and specialty and agricultural chemicals) accounted for two-thirds of the company's revenues, with only a third coming from energy. Most periodicals still classified Diamond as a chemical company.

Curiously, the company's move away from chemicals had occurred under the direction of a man who had risen from the chemical side of the business. The company's chairman and chief executive officer, William Bricker, had joined Diamond in 1969 as general manager of the Biochemicals Division. He then served as president of the Diamond Shamrock Chemical Company, was named chief operating officer of Diamond Shamrock Corporation in 1974, president in 1975, CEO in 1976, and chairman in 1979. That year he moved the company's headquarters from Cleveland to Dallas. When Bricker was named president, oil and gas sales constituted $309 million of Diamond's total sales of $938 million. By 1982, with a large increase in refining and marketing, sales and operating revenues from oil and gas totaled $1.78 billion. Revenues from coal amounted to $335 million and those from chemicals, $996 million or only 31 percent of the total.

Bricker had moved aggressively in his years atop Diamond Shamrock. *Chemical Week* magazine (June 1, 1983) reported that his associates had nicknamed him "J.R." in honor of the domineering television character; the article also noted that both his relocation of the corporate headquarters and his decision to move into the coal business were made in defiance of board members. I suspected early that the key to dealing with Diamond Shamrock would be in coming to terms with William Bricker.

The last four years had seen a marked expansion of Diamond's energy interests, beginning with the 1979 purchase of its first coal reserves, in Alaska, followed by purchases of two large U.S. mining companies, Falcon Seaboard Corporation and the Amherst Corporation. In July 1982 Diamond announced the purchase of Sigmor Corporation for $160 million, giving the company a second refinery and adding 600 self-service gas stations in Texas and Louisiana to the 1,100 stations it already owned. In the process, Diamond became the largest independent marketer in Texas. Its refining capacity jumped, meanwhile, from 40,000 to 110,000 barrels a day, although its own crude oil production was only about 10,000 barrels a day.

In search of oil to satisfy its refineries, the company stepped up prospecting off New Zealand and Australia, and in October 1982 paid $161 million for the right to explore on oil leases in the Beaufort Sea off Alaska, about forty miles northwest of the Prudhoe Bay field. Not everyone in the industry was as enthusiastic about the prospects and timing of these ventures as Diamond; the Diamond Shamrock booklet "The Beaufort Sea Story" quotes William Bricker, almost defiantly, "The conventional wisdom said, 'Global oil glut . . . trim your sails.' Diamond Shamrock responded with $161 million for five offshore Alaska leases." (That high-risk venture cratered with an expensive dry hole that prompted a $200 million write-off at the end of 1983.)

Reduced revenues from chemical operations resulted from general difficulties within that industry as well as from Diamond's divestiture, under Bricker's direction, of much of its chemical business, beginning in 1977. The Diamond Shamrock Chemical Company, which had retained its Cleveland offices, was brought closer to the parent company by consolidating operations at the Irving, Texas, headquarters of the industrial chemicals division. Most recently, in April 1983 the company had spun off one of its three chemicals divisions into a joint venture with Showa Denko, K.K., a Japanese chemical and pharmaceutical firm, to form an international agricultural chemicals and animal health business, and announced on May 20 agreement in principle with W. R. Grace and Company for sale of the second division, its process chemicals and metal coatings operations, to Grace for $140 million.

Even after the chemical divestitures, Diamond's chemical residues—literally and figuratively—posed difficulties. Several chemical facilities owned or previously owned by the company were reported to have released potentially hazardous materials into the environment. Three sites had been targeted by the Environmental Protection Agency for immediate remedial action. The company was potentially vulnerable to lawsuits and strained relations with the public. Suit was subsequently filed against Diamond in June concerning the discovery of dioxin at levels above those permitted by federal regulations at the former Diamond Alkali Company plant in Newark, New Jersey, where the company had manufactured herbicides.

Diamond Shamrock was already a co-defendant, along with six other major corporations that had manufactured the defoliant Agent Orange, in a class-action suit brought by some 15,000 Vietnam veterans and their families. The plaintiffs alleged that personal injuries, often long-lasting and difficult to treat, had resulted from exposure to Agent Orange during their military service. In 1980, several of the defendants, including Diamond, had moved for summary judgment on a government contract defense, asserting that they should be entitled to share in the government's immunity to suit, if any, since the government had dictated and controlled the circumstances surrounding the manufacture and use of the defoliant. The U.S. District Court for the Eastern District of New York ruled that a preliminary trial on that defense should be held, at which the principal issue to be decided would be whether, at the time each defendant produced Agent Orange, the government knew as much as or more than the defendant about the hazards accompanying use of Agent Orange. Trial on that issue was scheduled for June 1983. The District Court then combined that trial with one on the issues of liability and general causation. Diamond's liability would depend on the outcome of the trial. At the time of its tender offer for Natomas, Diamond faced a potential liability for billions of dollars in claims; Diamond managers could not have easily forgotten the recent spate of successful asbestos suits against Johns Manville that led the firm to declare bankruptcy. (In May 1984 the Agent Orange suits were concluded by an out-of-court settlement that resulted in no substantial material cost to Diamond Shamrock.)

It was easy enough to determine Diamond's prime interest in Natomas. The letter I received on Monday, May 23, from William Bricker said, in part, "The strengths of Natomas, together with those of Diamond Shamrock, would substantially increase the effectiveness with which both companies can operate in two exceptionally attractive and highly competitive energy markets, the Pacific Basin and the United States." Diamond's need for more crude oil was obvious: it was producing only 10,000 barrels of crude a day but could refine 100,000 barrels a day. To reduce the need to purchase the balance on the open market, it had announced more than a year earlier that it was interested in acquiring a company involved primarily in oil exploration and production. Acquisition of Natomas's Indonesian operations would nearly quadruple Diamond's existing crude oil reserves and would increase their share of daily oil production by approximately 50,000 barrels. In published reports Diamond officials stated that Natomas was attractive because 82 percent of Diamond's reserves were in natural gas, while 83 percent of Natomas's energy reserves were in crude oil; and 90 percent of Diamond's reserves were in the United States, while 90 percent of Natomas's reserves were overseas.

Diamond officials were also quoted as expressing interest in becoming more involved in the Pacific Basin, with its potential for economic growth. The Indonesian contracts and, conceivably, APL offered broader entrée into that region. We were concerned, though, that no one at Diamond Shamrock seemed to have much foreign experience, and none in Indonesia. We felt that the Indonesian contracts were solid in Natomas's hands, but were uncertain about Diamond's ability to maintain them.

Since Diamond was already successfully engaged in coal mining, a fit with the small Natomas coal operations seemed logical. I was sure the Geysers was a unique energy resource and an excellent investment, clearly a prize acquisition for a company seeking to diversify its energy holdings. We did not know, of course, whether Diamond would pay the price we believed these segments of the company to be worth, but at least Diamond's interest in them made sense.

We had a great many more questions about Diamond's intentions for APL and how highly they would value that business or the smaller real estate holdings. William Bricker's public statements about the proposed merger referred to a "powerful, integrated, and diversified international energy company" but said nothing about transportation or real estate. Speculation and rumors alleged that Diamond expected to sell off these assets, although one unconfirmed report suggested that Diamond wanted to retain APL in hopes of shipping coal from its Alaska field to Japan. We judged this a completely impractical idea for a number of reasons, among them that APL's ships were not coal carriers and that Diamond's Alaskan coal was of too low a quality to be competitive in the Japanese market.

We learned a little more Wednesday, when Diamond filed documents with the Maritime Administration (MarAd) declaring its intention to place APL in trusteeship with the Mercantile National Bank in Dallas if the takeover bid succeeded. Under that plan, Mercantile National would retain the dividends and distributions received from ownership of the APL stock. In Diamond's opinion this arrangement would avoid violations of the Merchant Marine Act, which forbids subsidized operators in foreign trade from having links with nonsubsidized domestic operators without Mar-Ad's permission. Diamond also indicated its intention to apply promptly for such permission as soon as the stock acquisition was completed. Among its shipping interests Diamond listed long-term charters to haul cargoes between ports on the Gulf of Mexico and the Atlantic and Pacific coasts, ownership or charter of liquid chemical barges operating between Gulf ports and ports on the Mississippi River and its tributaries, and ownership of open-hopper coal barges and towboats for moving coal between mines and ports on the Ohio River and its tributaries in the Cincinnati area.

The Merchant Marine Act also bars a change in control of a subsidized line without written permission from MarAd. Diamond submitted that the procedure it was suggesting would obviate the need for MarAd's approval of its domestic operations at the time it acquired the controlling interest it sought in Natomas, but requested that MarAd indicate its prior approval on this point. Nothing in these filings specifically indicated Diamond's long-term intentions toward APL, but the trusteeship proposal certainly sounded like a stopgap measure. Our contacts in Washington, D.C., corroborated our initial impression: Diamond did not, in fact, know what to do with the shipping interests.

If Diamond's plan to acquire Natomas made at least some sense, particularly on the energy side, the structure of the proposed deal did not. Natomas was carrying about $1.1 billion in long-term debt. Of that amount roughly $850 million was charged to Natomas Energy, about half of which was incurred during the prior year's purchase of Magma Power. The transportation company had approximately $270 million in debt, $100 million from purchase of its new ships and $170 million in obligations under capital leases. With slightly less than $1.1 billion in equity, Natomas's debt-to-equity ratio was slightly over 1-to-1, which we considered too high. I had left Occidental Petroleum ten years earlier partly because Armand Hammer wanted to keep expanding even once debt exceeded equity. I didn't think that was a good policy then, and I wasn't comfortable with it now.

The merger proposed by Diamond, however, would make Natomas's debt-to-equity ratio look like a model of conservatism. Diamond had long-term debt of nearly $1.2 billion, compared with its stockholders' equity of $1.45 billion. Now they were proposing to borrow at least an additional $700 million to purchase the majority interest in Natomas. Negotiations were likely to run the purchase price even higher. I doubted that Diamond's initial bid represented the best offer they were prepared to make. Thus, if the takeover succeeded, the new Diamond Shamrock would carry a minimum of $2.75 billion in debt, against $1.80 billion in equity. It looked like another Dome Petroleum,* not a deal we could recommend to the holders of the 49 percent of our shares who were going to end up with stock in Diamond Shamrock after the merger.

Diamond's bid now struck me as reckless. I could only assume that they planned to sell off some of the assets they hoped to acquire in taking over Natomas. Which assets I could only guess, but it appeared to me that they would be left with a very weak company. I couldn't possibly recommend that kind of deal to our shareholders.

---

*Dome Petroleum, a Canadian company, found itself in severe financial difficulty after a series of acquisitions for cash. Dome was seriously overleveraged, with a high debt-to-equity ratio, and was forced to the brink of bankruptcy.

· 8 ·

White Knights and
More Tender Tenders

At our meeting Tuesday afternoon, I told our assembled team that regardless of any of our hunches or preconceptions, we were going to consider every alternative. Our investment bankers, along with our own corporate development staff under the direction of Tom Neville, were to investigate every conceivable white knight. *White knight* is a picturesque shorthand term—no one buys someone else's company out of chivalry, and no corporate executive ever roamed the countryside assuming great personal risk to rescue innocents in distress. We were simply hoping to find a company interested in a deal that would seem attractive, even a bargain, on their own terms.

The Diamond Shamrock tender offer had set a floor on the price for Natomas and its assets. We were sure that the company was worth more, but we had to find someone who would agree with us and back up that assessment by offering a higher price than Diamond Shamrock had. Although for us, as Natomas's management, the ideal purchaser would also agree that the company would best be run in its present form and by its present team, this thought could play no major role in our decision. Price would rule. The efforts of some managements in recent years to thwart takeovers had led to what I considered rather bizarre behavior, frequently at the expense of their shareholders. More than one takeover target has defended its independence by selling off profitable operations at bargain prices; others substantially increased their debt by purchasing their own shares at inflated prices or hastily acquiring a new company or operation. Such companies thereby eluded their aggressors and managements kept their jobs, but often the companies were seriously weakened and the market value of their shares plummeted.

I knew that the value of Natomas warranted a vigorous search for a white knight, and we had already begun identifying likely prospects. Here our investment bankers played a crucial role, making inquiries among their clients, seeking responses from companies they knew or suspected might have an interest in Natomas, and evaluating the likelihood of our finding a compatible buyer.

Tully Friedman was blunt in insisting that I, as Natomas's CEO, had to make the principal contact with the CEO of any company that looked worth pursuing. CEOs respond to CEOs and are much more likely to listen to a fellow (or rival) executive than to an investment banker, who they suspect is simply looking for a fee. Besides, our situation was now well publicized; anyone I called would know that I was not interested in chatting just to pass the time of day. In a face-to-face meeting, I could quickly assess whether there was any real interest. We made a preliminary list of obvious candidates and started making calls.

We began with West Coast firms—Transamerica, Unocal, Arco, Southern Pacific, Pacific Gas and Electric—companies that might be interested in part or all of Natomas. The list, unfortunately, was not very long. All my calls received courteous, if noncommital, responses; under similar circumstances I would have behaved the same way. I set up a series of appointments for the next few days and assumed everyone would do some homework.

We had earlier decided to prepare material on the entire company and on each segment: the Indonesian oil and gas operations, the Geysers geothermal operations, APL, the domestic energy divisions, and our real estate business. Of these, the first three represented the bulk of our assets and earnings; they were obviously our most attractive holdings. By Wednesday we had packages of materials ready—information on historical earnings, forecasts, reserves, and projected ranges of value. Much as we disliked the idea, we knew we had to face the possibility, if not the probability, that Natomas as we had known it, as we had created it, would not survive. I was not about to break up the company simply to reduce its attractiveness to Diamond Shamrock, but I knew we had to consider a division or even liquidation if that would yield better value for our shareholders.

We also knew that if we elected to self-tender, to buy in some of our own shares at a higher but more realistic price than Diamond was proposing, we would have to sell part of the company to finance the deal. We could in no way guarantee that the company could or should be kept whole. That fact was uppermost in our minds as we looked at alternatives.

My first appointment was with Jim Harvey, the chairman and CEO of Transamerica Corporation, the sizable conglomerate (with assets exceeding $10 billion) headquartered in San Francisco. I gave Jim our package of material and suggested that since they were already in the transportation business, with Transamerica Airlines, and in the container leasing business—both related in one form or another to APL—there might be some strategic fit. I also suggested that acquisition of Natomas might offer a unique opportunity for Transamerica to enter the energy business.

Jim had come to the meeting accompanied by one of his associates whose principal responsibility was corporate development. The tone was friendly, but I did not see any real spark of interest. I was not surprised, therefore, when he called back two days later to say that, as he put it, "We have as much on our platter as we can handle at this time."

The newspapers, without any solid information to go on since we answered every inquiry with a "No comment," were busy reporting and following rumors. One of the more persistent rumors concerned Unocal Corporation (formerly Union Oil Company of California). These rumors seemed not implausible, since Unocal owned the other half of the Geysers and had substantial oil production in Indonesia. Fred Hartley, Unocal's capable outspoken chairman and CEO, was on my short list, but I considered him a long shot. I had outbid him for Thermal Power's 25 percent interest in the Geysers in 1974, and he had not challenged our bid for the other 25 percent owned by Magma Power in 1981. In fact, he had made it clear that he thought we had paid too much in both cases, a judgment I disputed. It seemed unlikely that he would now agree to pay an even higher price for our 50 percent of the Geysers.

Nonetheless, the rumors were rife. On Wednesday one enterprising *Wall Street Journal* reporter called Mary O'Neill, my executive assistant. The conversation went something like this:

> *Mary:* Mr. Common's office.
>
> *Male voice:* May I speak to Mr. Hartley, please.
>
> *Mary:* Mr. Hartley? I am afraid you have the wrong number. This is Natomas. Who is this, anyway?
>
> *Male voice:* I am . . . with the *Wall Street Journal.* I understand Mr. Fred Hartley is there meeting with Mr. Commons.
>
> *Mary:* Oh you jerk! [Click!]

The next day, the *Journal* dutifully reported that it was rumored that Fred and I had met Wednesday in San Francisco, although "a Unocal spokesman noted that Mr. Hartley had

been at the company's Los Angeles headquarters throughout the day."

I never did meet with Fred Hartley, although we had
several lengthy phone conversations between Wednesday
and Friday. I think he was intrigued, and to me it seemed
like a good strategic fit. The value to Unocal of acquiring
the other half of the Geysers was obvious. And with their
long and intimate involvement in Indonesia, they could be
far more comfortable with our Indonesian operations than
strangers to the area.

But I knew Fred's conservative nature. Our own evaluation of the Geysers was optimistic: projected annual earnings of $100 million by the end of the decade, perhaps
sooner. Without doubt it was a unique and long-lived energy asset, almost an annuity. Except under duress I would
not have sold it for less than $1 billion. But in that week in
May we were under considerable duress and might well
have to take substantially less.

On Friday, Fred Hartley called to say that Unocal had
decided there were other places they would rather put
their money. No, I was not surprised.

In the meantime, Salomon Brothers and Lazard Frères
were busy with their own calls—Superior Oil, Gulf Oil,
Santa Fe International, and many more—but had been
unable to elicit any solid interest. Ken Reed, our vice-
chairman, contacted British Petroleum. They were partial
toward the energy assets but couldn't even consider acquiring APL because of the MarAd restrictions on ownership of
United States subsidized carriers by foreign companies. Of
course, they could simply sell off APL. To enter into serious
discussions with British Petroleum, Jim Glanville, a Lazard
Frères partner, flew to London on Wednesday.

My most promising conversation, however, was on Thursday in San Francisco with Ben Biaggini, chairman and CEO
of Southern Pacific. Natomas had looked at Southern Pa-

cific as a possible merger partner in 1980. The logical fit we had seen then still remained. Southern Pacific, like APL, was a transportation company. In fact, APL was one of the U.S. railroads' largest customers, moving large numbers of containers by rail across the country, as well as into the interior. APL had been dealing with all the railroads that had routes to the West Coast—Union Pacific, Southern Pacific, Santa Fe, Burlington Northern—and it could make sense to tie one of these railroads into a single transportation network.

In addition, Southern Pacific was the largest private landowner in the states of California and Nevada, and some of those properties were likely sites for oil and mineral exploration. They were also in the real estate business, and some of our joint properties, such as those in Sacramento and San Francisco, were strategically located for future development.

In 1980 we completed an intensive, detailed study of a possible merger of the two companies. We had come very close to making a proposal but backed off when our railroad consultants produced a very bleak forecast for Southern Pacific's rail operations. After we dropped our investigation, rumors continued to circulate, which led to some spirited repartee between Ben Biaggini and me. Eventually, we became quite friendly.

In May 1983 Southern Pacific was closing the sale of its Sprint operation to General Telephone and Electric. The $800-million sale would leave Mr. Biaggini flush with cash. He was obviously intrigued by Natomas. I pointed out that there was not much time. Although he was on his way to the East Coast to close the sale of Sprint, he made an immediate call to his investment bankers, First Boston. By the weekend they were hard at work on the material in our offices.

On Friday I flew to Los Angeles for lunch with Bill

Kieschnick, the president and CEO of Atlantic Richfield Company (Arco), our partners in the Northwest Java Sea. We had a good relationship with Arco, although we had been pressing them for more rapid development of the contract area. My relations with Kieschnick had been friendly but not close. I scanned his face for any indication of interest. By my reading, Arco was not about to get involved.

By Friday our investment bankers had turned up a new prospect, American Petrofina, the domestic subsidiary of Petrofina, a Belgian company. I called Paul Meek, their chairman, and set up a meeting for Saturday. But I was neither very hopeful nor overly enthusiastic. Reportedly, they had shown interest in a number of other deals but had never completed one. I doubted that they would be very aggressive. Furthermore, American Petrofina was principally owned by the Belgian parent company; any stock trade would only dilute the position of the parent. By itself, American Petrofina was smaller than Natomas, not large enough to swing a cash offer without a substantial contribution by its parent. Paul Meek might, however, be interested in buying a piece of Natomas. On Saturday his team arrived in San Francisco to look at the Geysers and the domestic production. I met with them Saturday night, and on Sunday they were working in our offices when Bill Bricker and his Diamond Shamrock associates arrived to negotiate. We made no effort to hide the Petrofina representatives; their presence could only help our cause.

By Saturday night, I concluded that only one company, Southern Pacific, could possibly purchase all of Natomas, but we were a long way from negotiating a deal. No one else we had approached seemed up to the part of white knight. Negotiations with Southern Pacific would be time-consuming and precarious. Biaggini and I had not even begun to discuss a price seriously, although I'd told him that $30 a share or more would be necessary. But unless we could delay Diamond by legal impediments or otherwise, time was going to run out before we could make a deal with Southern Pacific.

Meanwhile, Tom Neville had been working with potential buyers of segments of the company, laying out for them our computer model projections and the basis for our estimates of future earnings and cash flow. Piecemeal liquidation would be a tough way to go, but, however painful, if it would net a better total price than either Diamond's final offer or the sale of Natomas to another bidder, we needed to consider it seriously. Sale of a portion of the company could also be used to aid a self-tender. By reducing the size of the company and adding the cash from the sale to our lines of credit, we could bid a higher price for our stock than Diamond was offering. Even if we were unable to make an immediate sale of assets, if we were sure that a sale would be forthcoming we could borrow the money for a self-tender and retire the loans with the proceeds from the later sale.

We were also aware that should we sell off choice assets, Diamond might be disinclined to purchase what was left and might withdraw its bid altogether. But any sell-off would have to leave us with enough of a company to justify the continued involvement of both management and shareholders.

Tom reported his findings throughout the week. Of Natomas's five segments—the real estate division, APL, North American domestic gas, oil, and coal operations, the Indonesian contracts, and our 50 percent interest in the Geysers—we quickly dismissed the first three as candidates for immediate sale. The real estate operations were too small to affect the outcome. In 1982, we had sold a 178-acre industrial site near Folsom, California, to the Intel Corporation for development of a manufacturing complex expected to employ about 10,000 people. In April 1983 we had sold our twenty-two–story San Francisco office building for $53.5 million to the California Public Employees Retirement System. Our remaining properties were in the Sacramento area and included the 936-acre Gold River development, the largest residential, office, and commercial project ever approved by Sacramento County. The project was attractive, but full development required a ten-year program, and any quick sale would yield insufficient cash to warrant the effort in the time we had remaining.

Our domestic energy holdings were relatively small and did not figure to be particularly attractive as a separate package. In the first quarter of 1983, the North American oil and gas operation contributed income of $3.3 million, compared with $5.1 million in the same period for 1982, the decrease due largely to lower domestic demand for natural gas. We had reported a loss of $66.6 million in our North American petroleum operations in 1982, compared with an operating income of $20.4 million in 1981. We had suffered a $75-million write-down of our U.S. petroleum producing assets, representing 18 percent of the company's domestic recoverable reserves, which at the end of 1982 stood at the equivalent of 29.1 million barrels of oil.

Weak market conditions had also eaten into profits from the coal operation, which contributed operating income of $800,000 during the first quarter of 1983, compared with $2.3 million during the same period a year earlier. We had closed three of our mines in 1982 and a fourth in April 1983. We figured our domestic oil, gas, and coal operations were worth around $300 million. But this was just not a propitious time to be seeking a purchaser for them.

We also decided that the timing wasn't right to hunt for a purchaser for APL, which was coming off a quarterly loss of $19.7 million (compared with an $8-million profit in the same quarter in 1982). Although we knew that the losses were the result of converging factors not soon likely to recur, we couldn't hope to find a buyer on short notice who would pay what we believed the operation to be worth. Any list of potential buyers for a U.S. flag line would be very short. The business is heavily subsidized and highly regulated by the federal government. A major oil company running its own tankers under foreign registry (sometimes called "flags of convenience" because of the liberal guidelines under which they operate) would be refused permission to acquire APL, since the owner of a U.S. flag line is forbidden from owning ships with foreign registry. So the chances of our suddenly finding a buyer seemed at best slim. The preliminary findings reported by Tom and the investment bankers confirmed our hunch, and we elected not to spend any more time on that idea.

Our Indonesian contracts were quite a different matter. We had come very close earlier in the year to selling an interest in our Southeast Sumatra contract to British Petroleum and also to a German oil company. We had hoped the sale would raise cash and reduce our debt position. But those discussions had collapsed, after fairly lengthy negotiations. In the wake of the Diamond tender, Ken Reed had gotten back in touch with British Petroleum, as I mentioned earlier. The restrictions that would complicate British Petroleum's purchase of the whole company (again, the APL ownership) did not apply to the petroleum operations. We reopened discussions but soon realized that we wouldn't have enough time to develop a satisfactory deal unless we could find a way to delay Diamond.

Our most serious discussions concerned the possible sale of the Geysers, which we regarded as an excellent candidate. It was a discrete interest, which could be separated easily from the rest of the company, and it was domestic. Geothermal power had a good reputation with the public as a clean, safe, and comparatively cheap way of producing energy with minimal environmental impact. But geothermal energy is practical only in a few places, and we had a 50 percent interest in the best. Our historical data supported our assertions, and our projections of profitability were excellent. All in all, the Geysers resembled an energy annuity that required little management by its owner since Unocal took care of operations.

We talked extensively with four prospective purchasers. Fred Hartley and Unocal had passed by the end of the week. Discussions with Petrofina, though inconclusive, were continuing. We also had very serious talks with PG&E and the California Public Employees Retirement System.

Since PG&E was already purchasing the output from our steam wells, direct ownership might be to their benefit. I met with Bart Shackelford, chairman of PG&E, on Wednesday in San Francisco. He was intrigued, but called back Friday to withdraw: as a public utility PG&E would face entangled and uncertain regulatory problems.

Our discussions with the California Public Employees Retirement System began with a call from Ken Cory, the State Controller, and an old personal and political friend. The state pension fund, with more than $20 billion in assets and income from employee contributions, and interest and dividends of $200 million a month, is a substantial investor. We had done business in April, when the Retirement System had purchased our office building. Ken had called early in the week, when he first heard about the Diamond tender bid, to offer assistance or advice. We discussed a number of possibilities, including the issuance by Natomas of a preferred stock with special voting rights. I was not sure that the pension fund could or should make such a purchase; and certainly they could consider doing so only if the investment could be demonstrated to be sound, prudent, and profitable. For Natomas a proposed sale to the Retirement System would be risky, virtually ensuring costly and protracted litigation. Nonetheless, I suggested that the

Retirement System look seriously at purchasing our interest in the Geysers. I believed a strong case could be made for the purchase since the operation required so little management and the property would produce a regular source of income for many years. Ken sent some of his people to San Francisco; they were still at work in our offices at week's end.

· 9 ·

Fighting Back

While scouting alternative purchasers, we also worked to fortify our defenses against the Diamond aggression. Even if we could not repulse the tender offer proceedings altogether, we knew that several of our other options, including most of the white knights, would take time to work out. We had to try to delay Diamond's purchase of our shares. We discussed briefly, but rejected, the Pac-Man defense, a ploy named after the video game in which figures rush about, trying to gobble up other figures before being eaten themselves. The strategy here, essentially, is for the target company to turn around and make a tender offer for shares of the very company that is trying to take it over. Pac-Man maneuvers have a certain appeal, naturally, to executives with a bent for combat (not to mention revenge), though their practical utility is somewhat more limited.

The most famous recent use of the Pac-Man defense was probably the Bendix–Martin Marietta brouhaha of 1982. William Agee, Bendix's colorful and controversial chairman, fired the first salvo by offering $43 a share for 45 percent of Martin Marietta, a Maryland-based aerospace and defense contractor, nearly 5 percent of whose stock he already owned. Five days later, the Martin Marietta board decided on a game of Pac-Man and offered $75 a share for just over 50 percent of Bendix's stock. Before that one was over, United Technologies, Allied Corporation, and half the investment bankers on Wall Street had joined in. But that, fortunately, is someone else's story.

Among the reasons we elected not to use Pac-Man was the simple fact that we did not really want to own Diamond Shamrock. We looked at the company and decided that it was not one we would have pursued in other circumstances. The chemicals operations were outside our expertise and held little interest for us, not to mention the company's pending liabilities in the Agent Orange and hazardous waste lawsuits. Diamond's domestic operations seemed a possible fit with our crude oil, but the general structure of the company, especially its level of indebtedness, was not attractive. We could justify a counteroffer only as a last-ditch defensive ploy to keep Natomas intact. Had we made a countertender and succeeded, the results might have been disastrous. We would have had to sell off assets to raise cash and doubtless borrow heavily besides. The effectiveness of the surviving entity would have been severely compromised. We agreed, therefore, to forgo the psychological gratification of a Pac-Man counterattack and to concentrate on more realistic options.

We were meeting each morning with counsel from Morrison and Foerster, the San Francisco firm we engaged after concluding that Joe Flom and Skadden, Arps would be able to advise us but would not actually litigate, should that be necessary. By Wednesday we were developing multiple lines of attack, and by Friday Morrison and Foerster were preparing a lawsuit for immediate filing in the likely event that we were unable to reach an agreement with Diamond. Most of these contingency plans were variations on one theme: allegations of Diamond's failure to disclose items that should have been disclosed or inadequate disclosure of items that were disclosed in its Offer to Purchase, Let-

ter of Transmittal, or SEC filings. The relevant federal law
states that:

> It shall be unlawful for any person to make any untrue
> statement of a material fact or omit to state any fact neces-
> sary in order to make the statements made, in the light of
> the circumstances under which they are made, not mislead-
> ing, or to engage in any fraudulent, deceptive, or manipula-
> tive acts or practices, in connection with any tender offer or
> request of invitation for tenders, or any solicitation of secu-
> rity holders in opposition to or in favor of any such offer,
> request, or invitation. (U.S. Code Title 15, section 78 n(e))

The SEC's mandate is neither to judge whether a transaction is good or bad nor to secure buyers or sellers from
making bad deals. Its concern is full disclosure, that the
public is fully informed about all aspects of a proposed
stock offering or transaction, including all its implications.
To satisfy this requirement, a security offering must be accompanied by a prospectus, which the company's lawyers
dutifully fill with warnings of all manner of impending dis-
asters. I would guess that if every prospective investor took
each clause of a prospectus to heart, few would proceed
with the purchase.

In any event, lawyers and investment bankers receive
healthy fees from securities transactions precisely for ensuring that the filings contain all the required "material" information. A primary defense strategy in response to an
unfriendly tender hinges on the ability of the lawyers for
the target company to produce long lists of alleged omissions and inaccuracies that, according to their argument,
are sufficient to void the transaction.

Part of the ritual of waging this sort of "dot-the-*i*'s" warfare is to charge the opposition with every breach of law,
regulation, and good manners you and your counsel can
imagine, and hope that enough of your arguments stand up

in court to force a temporary enjoinment that prohibits your opponent from acquiring or voting your company's shares. You then use the respite to prepare your next round of maneuvers. In preparing such a suit, the plaintiff's counsel casts a broad net to include anything that might catch the eye of the court. Since any determination as to which information is material is partly a matter of subjective judgment, we intended to produce everything we thought might be applicable.

By preparing to take legal action at this point, we were pursuing several goals. First, we might turn up information that would block the deal; highly unlikely, but nonetheless possible. And even if we could not block the takeover, we might delay the process and buy more time to stage a self-tender, seek white knights, find a more suitable purchaser for our company or its assets, or negotiate a better deal with Diamond.

We also felt that even the threat of a lawsuit might be enough to encourage Diamond to improve its offer. If we could raise the specter of the tender being judged invalid or indefinitely remaining in the limbo of litigation, the arbitrageurs might move on, either because our stockholders would sit out Diamond's offer in the hope of receiving a better one or because the arbitrageurs themselves would begin to doubt the odds of making a short-term profit off Natomas. To the degree that our shares remained in the hands of longer-term shareholders and out of the portfolios of the arbitrageurs, our ability to resist pressure for a settlement would be increased.

Morrison and Foerster, working with our staff people, prepared a comprehensive list of possible omissions or violations of disclosure requirements. Most important, for us, was the magnitude of the debt Diamond would be incurring under the offer as they had structured it. We were prepared to argue that they had not set forth adequately the implications of this debt for the future health of the company. Diamond was already carrying $1.2 billion in long-term debt; by assuming Natomas's $1.1 billion and borrowing at least another $700 million for the cash purchase of shares of Natomas, they would create a heavily over-leveraged new company.

This prospect had been forcefully emphasized on May 27, when Standard and Poor's, one of the nation's major credit-rating agencies, had announced that it was placing Diamond Shamrock on a "credit watch with negative implications" as the result of the tender offer for Natomas. This step is taken by the investment rating firms when they are concerned about the financial implications of a company's activities. Standard and Poor's advisory clearly signaled its concern and implied that it might lower Diamond's credit rating should the deal go through. A lower rating, of course, would mean the company would have to pay a higher interest rate for all its future borrowings. We could thus use the advisory to buttress our argument that Diamond had not adequately apprised the public, through its documents, of all the implications of the takeover bid.

We also intended to emphasize the effect on earnings of Diamond's borrowing so much money. The interest on the $700 million they proposed to borrow would cost the new company $65 million to $70 million a year. But the combined income of Diamond and Natomas for 1982 was only $229 million—the additional interest expense would have eroded profits by 30 percent. And in the first quarter of 1983 the combined companies had lost $1.9 million; a quarterly interest payment of $15 million to $17 million would have magnified that loss seven- to eightfold. Although Diamond could claim that the acquisition would produce efficiencies of scale that would offset some costs, this rebuttal seemed inadequate. We were sure we had grounds for claiming that this issue was both material and insufficiently disclosed in Diamond's documents.

The tax implications of the deal for our shareholders constituted another potentially troubling area. Everyone understood that Natomas shareholders who tendered their stock to Diamond for cash would be liable for taxes on their gains; but these shareholders would be receiving cash with which to pay the taxes. The question was whether the second tier of the Diamond proposal—the exchange of 0.92 shares of Diamond Shamrock stock for every share of Natomas not accepted for cash purchase—would be a tax-free exchange. Most straight stock-for-stock exchanges are not taxable; but under certain circumstances a transaction that involves cash as well as stock may be judged taxable in full. These matters are highly technical, and we could not be sure how the IRS would rule. But the possibility that the second-tier transactions would be taxable would obviously be of considerable concern to many Natomas shareholders, particularly if the merger was one over which they had no control. These shareholders would find themselves with new stock certificates but insufficient cash proceeds from the trade to ante up the taxes on the exchange. And it appeared to us that Diamond might have some incentives to structure the exchange as a taxable transaction. All this we believed had not been adequately disclosed.

We were also troubled by the language of the tender offer which promised only that, following consummation of the offer, Diamond "intended" to propose a merger with Natomas and to convert the remaining shares of Natomas to Diamond shares at the 1-to-0.92 rate. The wording left some real question as to whether they would ever take the second step. Diamond had also indicated that they might purchase more than the 30.4 million shares needed to gain control of Natomas, a move that seemed at odds with the intention to merge out the minority. If Diamond did not proceed with a merger, the remaining Natomas shareholders would be locked in to a minority position. The prospect of that uncertainty seemed to put undue pressure on shareholders to tender their shares immediately.

The SEC regulations do not require a tendering company to read the future or to promise to act in a particular way under all foreseeable circumstances. But they do require full disclosure of the company's present plans. We were prepared to argue that Diamond's intentions were inadequately expressed and therefore placed unjustified pressure on Natomas shareholders to tender prematurely.

During the week we conducted as thorough a review as time permitted of the class-action suit against seven chemical companies, of which Diamond Shamrock was one, that had manufactured Agent Orange for the U.S. military during the Vietnam War. The case already involved 960 lawyers representing some 5,000 veterans and 11,000 members of their families as initial plaintiffs, but judgments in the suit could be extended to apply to the millions of Americans who had served in Vietnam. Billions of dollars of claims and potential claims were involved. Diamond had supplied the military with Agent Orange between 1966 and 1968 and had disclosed its involvement in the litigation in its filings. But attorneys for the veterans had accused Diamond of destroying potential evidence, a charge Diamond vigorously denied. Our concern was real, and we would argue that Diamond's filings did not fully describe its potential liability.

We also determined that Diamond, like most chemical companies, faced potential lawsuits concerning its disposal of hazardous wastes. Time did not permit a detailed investigation, but our preliminary research revealed that at least ten of the chemical facilities currently or previously owned by Diamond had released toxic materials into the environment. At least three of these sites had been targeted by the Environmental Protection Agency for immediate remedial action. Again, we felt we might have grounds to allege insufficient disclosure.

All these issues could be raised in a legal action or as a rationale for advising our shareholders not to tender their shares, or at least to delay tendering, pending further disclosures by Diamond. Some shareholders, we believed, would be averse to owning stock in a chemical company whose environmental record was clouded. Certainly, our own doubts would have to be resolved before we could recommend any action to our shareholders.

Another area in which we questioned the adequacy of Diamond's disclosures concerned the $750 million credit agreement Diamond had made with its banks on April 15 "for purposes of acquisitions." They had also sold 3.1 million shares of their own common stock on March 23. We believed that both moves were calculated in anticipation of the unfriendly tender offer for Natomas, but that this intent had not been fully disclosed either in the prospectus for the public sale of stock in March or in the documents pertaining to a $250 million issue of debentures on May 4.

We were also prepared to question the heavy trading in Natomas stock during the week to ten days preceding the tender offer. The sudden surge in volume at least suggested that information might have been deliberately leaked to encourage the arbitrageurs to buy the stock, which would have aided Diamond's takeover effort. The New York Stock Exchange had already launched an investigation, as it does routinely when unusual trading patterns precede a tender offer announcement, but we wanted our attorneys to be prepared to raise this question in court. We knew we would be unlikely to prove any impropriety, but there had to be some explanation for the heavy trading in our stock immediately before their offer was announced, and that mystery might be judged sufficient grounds for enjoining Diamond from purchasing Natomas shares pending a more complete investigation.

Finally, we wanted our lawyers to scrutinize all the details relevant to the consent and approval of the Maritime Administration that would be required before effecting a change in the ownership of APL. To meet MarAd's restrictions on the percentage of ownership that may be held by foreign nationals, Diamond would have to disclose which portion of its shares were owned by overseas entities. Additionally, Diamond's proposal to place APL in trusteeship with the Mercantile National Bank might very well not be acceptable to MarAd; in any event, we felt we could probably delay that approval. Should any violation of MarAd regulations surface, the penalties could be severe, including loss of subsidy—up to $45 million to $50 million a year— which would make the transportation operation disastrously unprofitable.

In the relatively short time we had to prepare our briefs we were determined to make our case as strong as possible. We would outline the case and make our recommendations at the meeting of our Board of Directors set for Monday, May 30, Memorial Day. The Board would then decide how to respond to the Diamond Shamrock tender offer, and their decision would dictate the content of our Schedule 14D Statement to the SEC, which we would probably file the following day. In the event we elected to litigate, Morrison and Foerster were instructed to have a suit prepared for filing the first thing on Tuesday morning, seeking relief from the court by enjoining Diamond from acquiring or voting the shares until they had "corrected prior false and misleading statements," divested themselves of shares acquired in violation of regulations, and so on. The lawyers had their brief ready Saturday night. We believed that the probability of blocking the transaction seemed at best small; the chances of temporarily delaying Diamond's actions seemed somewhat rosier.

We were also reviewing our two contracts with the Indonesian government. These were our company's most important assets, by far the largest source of Natomas income, and certainly the crude oil reserves were the assets of most interest to Diamond Shamrock. As with all contracts with sovereign nations, we operated at the pleasure of the host government. We believed our relations with the Indonesians, carefully developed over a long period, were in good order, but we did not know how the Indonesians might react to a new operator.

We considered directly approaching Indonesian government officials to present our analysis that Diamond's offer could result in a financially weak company. But we concluded that approval by the Indonesian government might not be necessary, if the actual ownership of the contracts did not change. Nonetheless, the question of Diamond's future relationship with the Indonesian government could be critical. We knew that Diamond Shamrock had made an unfriendly tender for Tesoro Petroleum Company in 1980. In response, the government of Trinidad and Tobago, where Tesoro had a large refinery, announced that it would cancel its Tesoro contract in the event of the takeover. Diamond backed off. We also knew that Diamond had sent two top officials to Indonesia just prior to the tender offer to communicate their intent and give the Indonesian officials assurances about their plans. We did not know how those talks went, but we surmised that the Indonesians would remain noncommittal and await the outcome.

To approach the Indonesians before we had made any real decisions seemed risky at best. If we aroused the Indonesians' apprehensions only to then make a deal with Diamond, we could be stirring up a hornet's nest. Overtures to the Indonesian government at this point seemed unwise. I had several telephone conversations with Ed Masters, our senior vice-president for foreign relations and a former American ambassador to Indonesia, who was living in Singapore. We agreed that he should head for San Francisco immediately, and he was in my office by Thursday, prepared to leave for Indonesia should that become appropriate. In the meantime, he was close at hand, able to advise us on all matters that pertained to our conduct toward the Indonesian government.

· 10 ·

Negotiations

Bill Bricker had called me on Monday morning, the day after we heard about the tender offer. He said he wanted to conduct negotiations in a "friendly" way and would like to meet as soon as possible. I was irritated—a request for truly friendly discussions could have been made before launching the raid—and I saw no point in meeting him until we had assessed the offer and devised our strategy. When he phoned, his letter to me outlining the offer had just arrived. I said that we would consider the matter, and "You will be hearing from us."

During the week, however, it became clear that Diamond was very eager to talk. Their investment bankers at Kidder, Peabody were on the phone to Lazard Frères, our bankers, urging them to advise us to talk directly. We were still refusing public comment on their offer, hoping to keep them guessing. But rumors were rife. The press reported our expanding our line of credit, and talk of white knights persisted.

On Thursday Felix Rohatyn, who was in frequent contact with Kidder, Peabody, and I decided that we would be willing to talk to Bricker under certain conditions. First, the meeting would be held on our home ground, in our San Francisco offices. Second, we were meeting at their request, not ours; they were the ones who were anxious to talk, not us. This tactical position seemed to reflect the facts, although I knew it was in our interest to meet with Bricker and test Diamond's flexibility. As the aggressor, Diamond had fired the first shot, but we wanted to have the upper hand in any ensuing negotiations. Third, Diamond would have to increase the per-share price they were offering. Finally, the deal would have to be restructured on terms we deemed more reasonable. If they were unwilling to agree to these four basic conditions, there was no point in their coming to San Francisco.

We also let Diamond know that our Board of Directors would be meeting on Monday, May 30. The board meeting was essential, particularly if negotiations failed and we elected to defend ourselves. If the board agreed, we would file both our lawsuit and our Schedule 14D the next day. On Friday, Felix called back. Bricker and his associates had accepted our terms and would meet with us Sunday, May 29, in our offices in San Francisco.

I am sure that Diamond's strategy from the beginning had been to stun us with the tender offer and then calmly negotiate an agreement. But such transactions take on a life of their own once they begin, and the players sometimes lose sight of their original plan in the midst of moves and countermoves. Maybe they were more anxious to complete a deal this time around, after failing to acquire Tesoro Petroleum. How anxious they were we could only guess, and we guessed they were quite anxious. The Sunday meeting would be telling; for now, though, we knew they were willing both to raise their price and to restructure the deal.

Saturday, as our team gathered to review all the pertinent discussions and developments, our conversations continued with potential white knights and prospective purchasers of segments of the company.

The whole week had been one of acute intensity that at

times bordered on exhilaration. I am sure that I have remained in business for so long because I really enjoy the competition, the testing, and the excitement—particularly when I am in a position to make decisions of consequence. I could hardly have asked for more from a week than I was getting from this one.

And I was sleeping fitfully. In the early hours of Thursday morning I lay awake considering alternatives, proposing and responding in my mind to all sorts of variations on new offers we or Diamond might make. Then I began to play with a new concept—a spin-off. Instead of negotiating with Diamond for the whole company, why not negotiate for the segment they most wanted and retain the rest for Natomas shareholders? Diamond wanted our energy assets but didn't know what to do with our shipping line. They proposed to put APL in trusteeship with a relatively small Texas bank, and our Washington contacts had informed us that Diamond did not seem to understand APL, could not foresee how to handle it. We figured that soon after the takeover Diamond would try to sell both APL and our real estate interests, which were relatively small and unrelated to Diamond's other operations.

We knew from our analyses that APL was probably salable, and we were convinced that we had positioned APL for a return to profitability. But a quick sale was beyond reasonable hope. Potential purchasers were limited by MarAd's restrictions on foreign ownership, and U.S. flag operators would probably be barred by antitrust laws from acquiring a competitor. So I seriously doubted that we could complete a sale in time to prevent Diamond from acquiring Natomas. I was equally sure that Diamond, with little knowledge of the shipping company, would be unlikely to pay us what we felt APL was worth. In fact, Diamond might view our transportation business, with its $270 million in long-term debts and obligations, as a detriment, particularly after APL had reported a record loss for the first quarter of the year.

Why not spin off APL as a separate company that our shareholders would own under the present management or sell later under more favorable circumstances? Our shareholders would stand a chance of realizing a substantially better price for APL, and the spin-off would also simplify our negotiations with Diamond. We could then deal with the portion of Natomas that Bricker really wanted, the energy assets. Since APL was a discrete corporation, operated and financed separately from Natomas, it could easily be spun off, without the need for formulas to allocate debts or expenses. The principal disadvantage to APL from a spin-off would be that it would forfeit the tax shelter provided by Natomas oil operations. And, ironically, as an independent public company it could be vulnerable to an unfriendly takeover bid in the future. Otherwise, there was little standing in the way of a spin-off. Of course, I didn't want to break up Natomas, but circumstances were conspiring against our maintaining Natomas as we had built it. Given that, a spin-off seemed to be the best way to retain for Natomas shareholders the maximum long-term value from the shipping company.

The more I pondered this option, the more I felt I had found the key to turning the negotiations to our advantage. I arose Thursday morning, despite my lack of sleep, feeling as fresh as I had all week. I discussed the idea with Felix Rohatyn early that morning from my apartment, then with my associates as soon as I got to the office. We resolved to keep this option at hand as negotiations proceeded. Seaton suggested adding the real estate company to the spin-off. That made sense, too.

Felix Rohatyn and Jim Glanville from Lazard Frères arrived from New York for Saturday's meetings, as did Joe Flom from Skadden, Arps; Salomon Brothers was represented by Tully Friedman and his associates. We reviewed first our legal case and concluded that the chances of thwarting the takeover were fairly low, but the chances of delaying it for some indefinite period were fairly high.

Charlie Lee reported that he and his staff had commitments from ten banks for $1.2 billion in credit. We now had the muscle to seriously consider making a self-tender at a price that we considered more equitable for a sufficiently large portion of Natomas stock to force Diamond to raise its price or back off. Diamond was seeking 30.4 million shares; we figured we would need to buy between 20 million and 30 million shares to stop them. Our computer models and calculations had led us to a valuation in the range of $30 a share. The self-tender, then, would cost $600 million to $900 million. We had enough short-term credit, but we would be forced to sell assets to clear the debt. So a self-tender was simply the beginning of a liquidation. With all prospective buyers fully aware of our need to sell in a hurry, we hardly seemed likely to obtain the highest prices. For instance, we valued our interest in the Geysers at $1 billion, but if we had to sell it under the gun we couldn't expect to name our price. Fred Hartley had suggested a paltry $600 million, but I was sure we could do better if we had enough time.

Nonetheless, I was determined that $30 a share was a fair price. If we could not get an offer approaching that from Diamond or someone else, we ought to be ready to make a self-tender and a partial liquidation. Diamond's first offer of $23 in cash for half the stock and shares in a weakened company for the other half wasn't even in the ballpark.

We reviewed the white knight possibilities, an unfortunately short list. Southern Pacific was the most logical suitor, with over $800 million in cash available from their sale of Sprint to General Telephone and Electric, and a reasonably good fit between the companies in transportation.

Acquiring Natomas could offer Southern Pacific the opportunity to expand into energy on much the same basis as their arch competitor, Santa Fe. Mr. Biaggini and I had not seriously talked price, however, and knowing his cautious nature, I felt that any negotiations could take a long time, perhaps more time than we had. We were also still talking with American Petrofina, British Petroleum, and the California Public Employees Retirement System about purchase of some or all assets. I had not dismissed any of these options, but by Saturday night I felt that the most likely outcome would be a recommendation to our board that we file suit to delay Diamond and proceed with preparations for a self-tender.

Our first face-to-face meeting with Diamond Shamrock was set for ten o'clock Sunday morning. In addition to our principal officers, we had an on-call list of home or hotel phone numbers for most of the key people from each of our divisions, including those who were traveling or on vacation out of the country, and even a ship-to-shore number and a code name for reaching Tom Baker, president of Natomas Real Estate Company, somewhere in the middle of Lake Shasta. Mary O'Neill had arranged for a team of secretaries and switchboard operators to be available all weekend; she had datafax operators in the office and telex operators on call. We had the air conditioning system turned on for the weekend and arranged for food to be delivered to the Captain's Cabin, a private dining room in the building, and to the conference room on the seventeenth floor.

This was the Sunday of a holiday weekend, but the building was anything but quiet. In addition to our own staff of management personnel, attorneys, accountants, the corporate development group, and support personnel, our investment bankers and outside counsel were also present. We had provided office space for the representatives of the various groups with whom we were dealing, American Petrofina, Southern Pacific, and the California Retirement System. All of them were busily at work when the Diamond Shamrock team arrived. Since everyone had to sign in with the guard on the ground floor, it probably didn't take much effort for Bricker and his associates to note who was already there. We assumed it wouldn't hurt for them to know that they were not our only visitors.

We met in our boardroom. The Diamond principals were William Bricker (CEO and chairman of the board), J. L. Jackson (president and chief operating officer), and J. Avery Rush, Jr. (vice-chairman of the board). Ken Reed, our vice-chairman, and Bruce Seaton, president and chief operating officer—positions that both had just assumed—and I constituted the Natomas management team. In addition, Joe Flom, Felix Rohatyn, Jim Glanville, and Tully Friedman were on our side of the table. Diamond's support group included Marty Lipton and Marty Siegel. The last Sunday in May found some of the most experienced merger and acquisition lawyers and investment bankers in the country in our boardroom.

I opened the meeting by outlining our position. I reminded everyone that I planned to make my recommendations at the next day's board meeting. As part of our review of all our options, I wanted to be sure that we had explored the possibilities of working out a deal with Diamond Shamrock. I rejected their first offer as "totally inadequate." I also said, candidly, that I was not sanguine about the prospects of our coming to an agreement, because I suspected that the two sides had disparate notions of Natomas's value. That might have sounded like a bluff, but it was not. I did not expect to reach agreement before the board meeting. When I asked Bricker for the basis of their $23 bid, he promised to provide the details. And I reiterated why the structure of the deal they were proposing was unacceptable: borrowing money to repurchase equity would create a financially crippled company. We simply could not recommend to our shareholders that they accept stock in such a company. We were willing to look at a different proposal, but time was short.

During the course of these introductory remarks, Ken Reed, Bruce Seaton, and I were quietly assessing our opponents. I am sure they were doing the same. They were the essence of civility. Bricker, a large man, was clearly in charge. He did most of the talking. It is certainly difficult to read a man during a first meeting, but we were all experienced in such encounters. We had never met the Diamond management team, and "reading" them correctly was vitally important to our negotiating position. Jackson said little and showed little emotion. But Rush was voluble, responding smilingly or knowingly to my comments and echoing or embellishing on Bricker's statements. He oozed sincerity and concern. I put it down to posturing. Bricker was more difficult to read, but he seemed anxious to keep the meeting friendly. Ken and I exchanged glances. I think we simultaneously had the same gut reaction: Bricker had come to make a deal.

Now the maneuvering began. I was not prepared to make a specific counteroffer just yet. For one thing, I didn't want to set a ceiling on any terms that early in the negotiations, which my associates and I assumed would extend, with interruptions, over several days. Furthermore, our attorneys had advised us that if we made any specific proposal we would be required to divulge it in our Schedule 14D filing, since the SEC would probably construe a counterproposal as material information to which the public was entitled. We were not yet prepared to go that far. Besides, we had told Bricker why his proposal was unsatisfactory. I wanted to see how he would respond.

Our attorneys now proposed one of those legal niceties of the corporate world that would free us from having to prematurely disclose counteroffers made in direct negotiation: "conversations" would be carried on between the investment bankers representing their respective clients. Investment bankers are able to sound each other out without speaking directly for the principals. One banker could say, "I am willing to recommend this," and the other banker could counter with, "If you did, then I might recommend that." So long as the investment bankers were talking and the principals themselves were not, no immediate disclosure would be required. If those conversations succeeded in leading to an agreement between the principals, then only that agreement—and not the interim moves—would have to be disclosed.

In one sense, it seemed like a very expensive approach, at the rates both sides were paying their lawyers and bankers—but it worked.

Before the principals adjourned, I did say (in general terms, avoiding any specific proposal) that we would almost certainly look more favorably on an equity deal, an exchange of stock for stock, rather than a deal that also involved cash, and that we favored a spin-off of APL and the real estate business as part of any deal with Diamond Shamrock.

We then dispersed; the investment bankers went off together, while Reed, Seaton, and I went to my office to compare notes, assess our adversaries, and await some report from our bankers. At noon our group went to lunch in the Captain's Cabin, where we continued our discussion, getting reports from time to time from the bankers' conclave.

I had no strong feeling about how things were going, until Jim Glanville was called out and returned with a message from Bill Bricker. Bricker's tidings were succinct: "I want to get rid of the damned bankers and lawyers. I think I can make a deal with Commons. See if he is agreeable to a one-on-one meeting between us." "Fine," I said, "I'll be prepared to meet alone with Bricker at two o'clock."

That certainly added spice to the rest of our luncheon discussion. Our bankers were reporting that Diamond was prepared to restructure the deal. They should have been, since making a cash tender had been a ridiculous idea from the beginning. Shifting to an equity basis was as much in their self-interest as in ours. Fortunately, they recognized that.

Much of our table talk now centered on price: How much additional value might Diamond be willing to add? What were we willing to accept? Once Bricker and I began negotiating directly, we would be accountable through the disclosure requirements, so I had to be sure about our objectives. We disagreed among ourselves as to the minimum price we should be willing to accept. I remained convinced that if we had enough time to carry out a liquidation, we ought to be able to realize something in the neighborhood of $30 a share. I wasn't prepared to settle for less.

We had surmised that they had arrived at their offer by taking the market price of Natomas, which was trading at $15.50 before the tender rumors, and adding a 50 percent premium, a fairly standard formula designed to make the offer seem irresistible to shareholders.

The next report from our investment bankers contained the intelligence that Bricker's new proposal would be a straight share-for-share exchange, one to one. With Diamond stock having closed the previous Friday at $23.75, this new bid was essentially the same as their original one, except that now they were offering stock instead of cash and wanted the whole company, not 51 percent. That wasn't an improvement.

By proposing an equity transaction, we had somewhat boxed ourselves in. We knew that the new combined company would be stronger, since Diamond wouldn't be taking on new debt to buy us out, but we were also entering uncharted territory. Our complete information about the value of Natomas's assets and liabilities was confronted by our minimal information about Diamond. For obvious reasons we had not had time to appraise Diamond's assets in any depth, and we had qualms about their potential liabilities. Of course, if their current market price was considerably below actual or realizable value, as was the case with Natomas, then conceivably an all-equity deal could be quite advantageous. But without detailed appraisals, we had to judge the value of the equity deal on the market price of Diamond stock alone.

It was not the first time in my business career that I had to make a decision based on incomplete information. But I knew I could not accept the equivalent of $23 or $24 a share for Natomas. There was a general consensus at our table: the one-for-one offer was as far as Bricker would go that day, but he would quite probably be back in the morning. That might make for an interesting night tonight. If Bricker was as determined to make a deal as Reed and I suspected he was, he would have to considerably revise his most recent offer. I expected our two o'clock meeting to be a short one.

I had also decided by then that the spin-off of APL and the real estate company to our shareholders had to be part of the deal. We'd never get the full value of those assets out of any trade with Diamond. Our valuation of those two groups of assets was about $300 million, or between $4 and $6 per share of Natomas. (As it turned out, our estimate was proved conservative.)

Assuming Diamond accepted the spin-off, we would then be dealing for the energy assets alone. Since I did not believe that Diamond assigned much value to the assets we proposed to spin off, certainly not the $4 to $6 a share we estimated, I felt there was a reasonable chance that we could still trade Natomas stock for Diamond stock in the same range of one-for-one. And, in fact, when Bricker's associates tried to explain to our bankers how they arrived at their $23 bid, we could see that APL didn't count for much in their calculations.

I hardly expected to get close to a substantive agreement that afternoon, but we needed to decide among ourselves what terms would be acceptable. With Diamond selling for just under $24 and the spin-off of APL yielding another $4 to $6 a share, the one-for-one exchange and the spin-off would yield $27.75 to $29.75 per Natomas share. Each tenth of a share more of Diamond that we could negotiate into the exchange ratio would add $2.375 to the amount our stockholders would receive for each share of Natomas. Despite the ease of making the proper calculations, so far we were negotiating with ourselves. I had no reason to believe that Bricker was prepared to come even close to our figure.

At two o'clock Bricker entered my office and sat down at one end of my couch. I sat at the other. After a few pleasantries, he made his offer of one share of Diamond, the new combined company, for each share of Natomas. No surprises there, our intelligence had been correct. I assumed the meeting was about over: "Mr. Bricker, we are no closer at this point than we were before we started. I don't think there's much point in continuing these discussions." He started to get up. Then he sat back down. "What kind of a deal would you make?" he asked.

I took my time replying. I was not surprised that he was asking for a counterproposal. But I expected that my offer would bring the negotiations to a standstill, at least temporarily. He would certainly listen to my proposal, but then he would walk out, in disbelief or frustration, since my proposal valued each Natomas share $6.375 to $8.375 higher than his revised offer. Or he would politely reject our counterproposal, I would politely thank him for coming, and our team would proceed to work on other strategies and await the next day's developments.

"I am prepared to recommend to my board that we accept an arrangement in which we spin off APL and the real estate operations to our shareholders and exchange the balance of Natomas for 1.1 shares of Diamond stock for every share of ours."

Then he surprised me. Instead of a pro forma refusal, he said, "Let me go downstairs, I want to discuss this and run some figures, and I'll get back to you as soon as I can."

We had provided them with space in the building to work, and we left them alone. My associates rejoined me after Bricker had gone. They were genuinely surprised. Ken grinned. Bricker *had* come to make a deal. I thought it was too soon to tell; I didn't want to get up any false hopes. There was no question that Bricker's response was far more positive than any of us had anticipated. We agreed that he was probably prepared to concede the spin-off. The real guessing game lay in the exchange rate, but his attitude and his willingness to look at the numbers again suggested that he was ready to sweeten his last offer. I guessed that he would accept the spin-off and propose a one-for-one exchange ratio for the stock. We each thought that such a proposal would be tough to turn down. The yield to our shareholders would range between $27.75 and $29.75 a share, depending on the value of APL. We were getting close to our target price of $30.

We passed several hours discussing, debating, and trying to second-guess what Bricker's team was doing. We later learned that they had been getting computer runs from Dallas, but the computer had broken down. So while we were spinning complex hypotheses about their counter-counterproposals, they were just trying to get their computer to work.

While we awaited Bricker's return, we also reviewed with our attorneys the other matters that would have to be addressed if in fact we reached agreement on the main terms. We were concerned about the future of Natomas's employees in the event of a merger. We agreed that any contracts or arrangements regarding the officers could not be discussed or raised as a condition of the agreement because of a possible conflict of interest. But the employees were another matter; I intended to provide as much protection for them as possible. Our first responsibility, however, was to our stockholders.

At half past four Bill Bricker sent word that he was ready to meet. He came into my office carrying a handwritten sheet of paper, and asked that I have copies made of it, which I did immediately. He then suggested that we go through his list item by item before I gave my response. I agreed, and we reviewed the list together:

1. *"Common stock merger. Tax Free. Purchase—not pool—accounting."* I saw no problem here. We wanted an exchange of common stock for common stock, a tax-free exchange for our shareholders. Diamond was concerned about the possible tax consequences of the spin-off, and wanted our cooperation in structuring that part of the transaction. In this case, our interests were identical. The matter of purchase versus pool accounting did not concern us, but appeared to be important to them. How an acquisition is treated for accounting purposes, however, is really governed by accounting rules, not by agreement. Since they would be paying a substantial premium over Natomas book value, they wanted to reflect that premium in the valuation of the assets.

2. *"Exchange ratio: one Diamond share for one Natomas share. No collar. No adjustments for change in market prices. No matter what happens, exchange ratio remains one to one."* That was the ratio I had anticipated; we would have to talk about it later, when we had completed the list. It was one of two key items. If we could agree on the ratio and the spin-off, I suspected we could reach agreement on the other provisions. The "no collar" and the fixed rate could be worrisome. Merger agreements often provide that if the price of the purchasing company's stock goes above or below a certain "collar" level, say $2 or $3 either way, before the date of the actual exchange of shares, there will be an adjustment in the exchange ratio. If we agreed to this provision, a substantial drop in Diamond's stock price could leave our shareholders vulnerable, or it might lead them to reject the merger. This was a chance we might have to accept if all our other major objectives were reached.

3. *"Spin-off of APL to Natomas shareholders—probably tax free."* That was the big jump. With Bricker agreeing to that, I knew we were close to a deal. I inserted "and real estate" on the sheet to clarify what we had previously proposed through the bankers. Bricker agreed. There was a question as to whether we could successfully structure the spin-off as a tax-free exchange to Natomas shareholders. (We subsequently were successful.) But since that part of the deal represented only about 20 percent of the total transaction, and as long as the other 80 percent was tax free, I was prepared to go ahead.

4. *"Definitive merger contract signed Monday night."* We had already advised Diamond that unless the tender offer was withdrawn Tuesday morning, the next working day, we intended to file our lawsuit. Bricker didn't want to withdraw the tender offer unless he had a signed contract. I was agreeable, provided the attorneys could get the work—a tremendous amount of work—done that night, so that the agreement could be approved by our Board of Directors. I learned later that Bricker evidently had a very broad mandate from his board; he did not need to obtain its approval of the revised agreement before signing it. That was a broader mandate than I had, or would have wanted to have.

5. *"No fairness opinion conditions."* By accepting this

provision, we would be forfeiting the right to demand a later evaluation of the fairness of the agreement from experts such as our outside investment bankers. We would be pledged to live with the agreement we had made, even if we later judged that agreement to be unfair. If we wanted a fairness opinion we would have to have it before we signed an agreement with Diamond. Our investment bankers were prepared and did provide a fairness opinion to our Board of Directors the next day. There was no equivocating; both investment banking firms judged the deal as fair to our shareholders.

6. *"Merger contract to contain only basic financial representations, and no material adverse change conditions."* With regard to Natomas's basic financial representations, I had no problem. But I wasn't as certain about the financial representations of Diamond. I wanted Natomas to have the right to conduct a due diligence review of Diamond Shamrock's operations; if there were material misstatements or omissions in the financial statements that Diamond had already filed, such misstatements or omissions would constitute a condition under which Natomas could back out of the deal. We subsequently reworded this item to give Natomas, but not Diamond, this right.

7. *"Natomas convertible preferred to remain outstanding. Use new holding company structure."* Natomas had 25 million shares of a cumulative convertible preferred stock outstanding. Preferred stock differs from common stock in two ways. First, preferred stock is entitled to a fixed annual dividend ($4.00 a share in our case) that must be paid before dividends can be paid on the common stock. Second, in the event of liquidation of the company the preferred shareholders receive the stock's par value ($50 a share in our case) before any payment is made on the common shares. Natomas preferred stock was also convertible into Natomas common shares (at 0.9303 common shares for

each share of preferred), but with Natomas common stock paying a much smaller dividend and selling at a lower price in the market, preferred shareholders had no incentive to convert. Each share of preferred stock could also be redeemed at the company's option at $53.20 a share. While some companies' preferred shareholders constitute a separate class of shareholders, who must separately approve all company merger transactions, our preferred shareholders did not have that right, though some holders later went to court to argue otherwise.

Bricker proposed that the convertible preferred stock remain outstanding in what would become the Natomas subsidiary of Diamond Shamrock. I could accept that, provided Diamond was prepared to adjust the conversion rate to reflect the spin-off; they were. Under the agreement, then, our preferred shareholders would continue to hold the same rights and receive the same dividends as before. (When litigation was later threatened by a group of preferred stockholders, Diamond agreed to offer a new Diamond convertible preferred stock with improved terms and conditions in exchange for the then-outstanding Natomas preferred shares. The exchange required the approval of a majority of the total convertible preferred shares; it was approved at the special shareholders meeting in August 1983.)

8. *"Natomas to name two Diamond directors. Present Natomas board to continue as members of Natomas subsidiary board."* Diamond's board had twelve members. I thought that since Natomas shareholders were going to own almost half of the new company, two directors were not sufficient. Bricker was friendly. "How many do you want?" "Four." He paused and thought a moment. "Well, I'm trying to keep down the number of inside directors" (inside directors are those who are also employees or officers of the company). I said, "Fine. We'll name two inside and two outside directors." That seemed to satisfy him.

9. *"No adverse changes in Natomas benefit plans."* This met one of my concerns. Natomas had a well-constructed package for its employees—health, pensions, and other benefits. Diamond was agreeing to keep it intact or provide substitutes that were as good.

10. *"All existing employment and severance arrangements honored."* I said that I could not discuss this matter until we had reached agreement on the basic terms, that until I knew we had the best possible deal for our shareholders, I would not discuss matters that might apply essentially to Natomas management. He understood. Later I would make a strong case that the continuity of management and the organization were important to the interests of Diamond and to the shareholders. But that argument would have to stand on its own merits. It was not a condition of the agreement.

11. *"Natomas stock options rolled over or cashed out."* In the past nine years we had issued a significant number of stock options to our key employees under a plan established with shareholder approval. Some 140 officers and key employees in positions that affected the profitability of the company had been given stock options. Since Natomas common shares would not exist once the merger took place, Diamond was proposing that these options either be reissued as Diamond share options or be cashed out. This proposal was quite acceptable to me.

12. *"Diamond will have the right to tender for Diamond shares as in Morton-Thiokol merger."* I didn't know precisely what they had in mind, but they later indicated that they wanted the right to buy for cash up to $300 million of their own shares. I cautioned against such a move because of its negative impact on their balance sheet, but we agreed to the provision. I suspected they wanted to be able to support the price of Diamond shares in the event of their weakening in the market. Fortunately, they never availed themselves of that option.

The list covered the main issues, and I was sure the lawyers would translate it into an agreement. The structure of the deal followed our proposal. I was pleased, but we were not quite there. I looked at Diamond's CEO. "Mr. Bricker, I think we're close to a deal, but I'm not prepared to recommend it to my Board of Directors. I will discuss it with my associates, and we'll make up our minds whether to take it to the Board tomorrow." After an appropriate pause, I added, "However, if you want a deal right now, I'm willing to make one—I'll make it on the basis of the spin-off and a 1.05-to-1 exchange of stock."

The difference between a 1-to-1 exchange of 55.8 million shares at $24 and a 1.05-to-1 exchange was worth $66 million to our shareholders. Bricker looked at me for a moment without saying anything. Then he started to rise, hesitated, and stuck out his hand. We had a deal.

We had come a long way, much farther than I had thought possible in so short a time. Diamond had agreed to pay $2,350 million for the Natomas assets that they were acquiring: common stock with a market value of approximately $1,400 million, preferred stock worth $100 million, and assumption of long-term debt of $850 million. My analysis showed that we would be receiving values at the upper end of the range for the individual segments of the company: $1,000 million to $1,200 million for Natomas's Indonesian holdings, $800 million to $1,000 million for the Geysers geothermal properties,* and $350 million for the balance of the assets, principally domestic oil, gas, and coal, and net working capital.

Most importantly, with the added value of the APL and real estate spin-off our common shareholders' position had

---

*I do not know how Diamond allocated the purchase price, but I can only assume that it differed from my evaluation. Late in 1984 Diamond announced the sale of one-half of their interest in the Geysers geothermal properties to Unocal for $285 million.

been improved by $6 to $8 a share over Diamond's original offer, or by as much as $400 million, to a total value of approximately $1,700 million.

At $30 a share, the value of our stock had doubled compared with its market price two weeks before Diamond's tender offer was announced. I did not believe that we could do better.

·11·

"The time has come . . ."

With that handshake, I had agreed to the termination of Natomas as a public company. The newspaper reports over the next few days expressed surprise that we had reached an agreement so quickly and that we had not resisted Diamond longer. It had surprised me, too, that we had been able to obtain our objectives so quickly. I had fully expected to be preparing for a self-tender or filing a lawsuit and pursuing other alternatives. I was quite prepared to walk away if the terms were unacceptable, and I think Bill Bricker knew that. I also think that Ken Reed and I were right in our initial impression on Sunday: Bricker had come to make a deal.

I don't know how much Bricker was influenced by his investment bankers. Bankers are hardly disinterested parties; in a tender offer they stand to earn substantially higher fees if the deal is consummated than if it falls apart. However, Bricker had a reputation as a very independent man; I suspect he made his own decision. At any rate, he acted quickly and decisively, and I was satisfied.

In addition to the price, we had other reasons to recommend the agreement as in the best interest of our stockholders. The deal had been structured to produce a new Diamond that would have about $3 billion in net worth against \$2.0 billion in debt, substantially better than Diamond's original proposal that would have resulted in a company with almost the reverse ratio of debt to equity. So our shareholders would be receiving shares in a financially strong company. Moreover, we had traded our stock at our appraised value for their stock at market value. As a result, our shareholders would own a proportionally larger share of the combined companies: Natomas would be contributing, at book value, 37 percent of the total assets of the new company (along with about 41 percent of the liabilities), but Natomas shareholders would hold 58.5 million, or more than 46 percent, of the 126.5 million shares of common stock in the new Diamond.

If we were going to submit a formalized agreement for the Natomas board's approval on Monday, Bricker and I agreed that the attorneys and everyone else had to get to work right away. I returned to my associates and reviewed our understandings. The drawing up of the documents began. This kind of transaction is incredibly complex, even after the parties have agreed in principle. The proxy statement that was subsequently mailed to Natomas and Diamond Shamrock shareholders ran to 187 pages of text, 128 additional pages of financial statements, and 82 pages of exhibits. The attorneys and staff worked all night, and the agreement, though not the exhibits, was ready in time for the Monday morning board meeting.

Once the attorneys were at work on the agreement, Bricker and I met for another twenty to thirty minutes to discuss employees and contracts. I had decided earlier in the week to propose to our Board Executive Compensation Committee contracts for a key group of our top- and middle-management people who did not already have such arrangements. As the week progressed I had become increasingly concerned about the continuity of our organization and what could happen to Natomas during a long, drawn-out battle or an uncertain transition period. Had we decided to resist the takeover, even if we were successful, we might lose key personnel to more stable competitors. Four of us (myself, Ken Reed, Bruce Seaton, and Charlie Lee) had contracts, most in place for several years, but key managers without contracts were running important operations, and I was afraid we might lose them in a takeover or during protracted negotiations or a period of uncertainty.

Earlier in the week I had called a special meeting of the Executive Compensation Committee for Monday morning, May 30, prior to the meeting of the Board. I would ask them to consider drawing up contracts for fifteen officers and managers.

I must admit that the threat of a takeover had changed my attitude toward employee contracts. I used to view them as largely for the benefit of the employee, not the company. But the external threat changed all of that, and suddenly the issue was no longer an abstract matter. Samuel Johnson once commented that "when a man knows he is to be hanged in a fortnight, it concentrates his mind wonderfully." Without straining the analogy, I must say that the imminent threat of a takeover sharply focused my attention on preserving our organization.

Much has been written about "golden parachute" employment contracts. In their most appropriate form, a golden parachute contract protects a key employee, for example the CEO or another vulnerable associate, by providing employment or income guarantees in the event of a takeover. These contracts protect the shareholders as well, because they permit key officers to respond objectively to a takeover threat, to negotiate without fear about the effect on their personal futures. Such contracts should be distinguished from those—which are more appropriately called "golden handcuffs"—written primarily to preserve the continuity of an organization.

From the beginning of the battle, my top associates and I felt secure in the knowledge that regardless of the outcome we would be protected by our contracts. My contract, as modified over the years, had been in effect for almost a decade. It was set to expire in 1989 but could be terminated on three years' notice. The other officers' contracts were terminable on one to three years' notice. I had no illusions about my role in the new Diamond: no company has room for two CEOs. But my contract enabled me to ignore the personal outcome and devote all my effort and energy to negotiating the best deal for our shareholders and employees. That's the way it should be.

The terms of a target company's golden parachute contracts, unless negotiated in haste in the middle of a takeover battle, are known to the aggressor and seldom represent a significant enough liability to deter or even affect its thinking. Of course, a contract so generous as to constitute an incentive to an officer to sell the company at any price would be disastrous; but no responsible board of directors of a public company would approve that kind of arrangement. One way or another, managements are going to look, at least in part, after their own self-interests. Having observed the price some managements have paid to maintain their positions—either in the form of greenmail or sale of their companies to tarnished white knights, or in the emasculation of their company by the sale of prime assets—I would argue for contracts sufficiently generous to allow officers to negotiate objectively, freed from overriding concerns for their own futures.

Golden handcuff employment agreements are equally essential to protect the company. A takeover attempt can become a long-running show, especially when several parties enter the bidding or when the battle degenerates into lengthy litigation. Even friendly negotiations can take weeks or months, and in those instances key personnel, who may not be directly involved in the negotiations, are at best still distracted from doing their jobs. At worst, they may start looking elsewhere for positions that hold the prospect of longer tenure. To keep these people on the job, contracts that offer some measure of protection benefit the company as much as the employees.

Once a takeover is about to be concluded, both companies benefit by providing incentives for the acquired company's employees to remain on the job during the transition period, at least until an assessment can be made. Merging two organizations is difficult enough, and wholesale terminations and uncertainty about tenure only compound the problems. Hasty personnel actions can be disastrous, particularly if the acquiring company does not have expertise in the field of its new acquisition. Employment contracts or other incentives that discourage or at least slow layoffs and attrition serve a valuable function.

When Bricker and I met again late Sunday, he stated that he wanted any new contracts or contract changes to be approved by the Natomas board the next day so that these terms would be set by the time the final agreement document was to be signed. That was fine with me.

My first request was that for two years after the merger any Natomas employee released as a result of the merger be given a lump-sum six months' severance pay. I was unaware that any similar provision had ever been included in a merger agreement, but I believed it was important. Although most companies do make provision for their top officers, hundreds of employees affected by a merger are frequently left to fend for themselves. I did not see how we could negotiate on behalf of the shareholders and the management but leave the rest of the employees hanging.

Bricker agreed: Any Natomas employee (except employees of APL and the real estate company and a few others, such as coal company employees covered by union contracts) would receive six months' severance pay if he or she were terminated without cause within two years of the merger, or were required to relocate, or suffered reduction in salary or benefits or a change in duties or responsibilities. Next we took up the matter of Natomas's officers and key managers. I asked that contracts be drawn up for those key people who had been working without one and that the contracts in force be revised. The discussion was interesting. I suspected that I would have little trouble getting contracts for those people key to the company.

Earlier we had reviewed Diamond Shamrock's SEC filings and found that they had termination agreements with fourteen of their top executives, including Bricker, which provided for *ten years* of compensation in the event of a "change in control" of the company. These provisions were somewhat unusual and are worth quoting at length from the Diamond-Natomas proxy materials:

> A change in control of Diamond Shamrock is deemed to have occurred (i) upon a change of a nature that would be required to be reported in a proxy statement filed under the Exchange Act, (ii) when any person becomes a beneficial owner of 25 percent or more of the voting power of Diamond Shamrock or (iii) when during any period of 24 consecutive months individuals who were directors at the beginning of such period cease to constitute a majority of the Board of Directors. In such an event, the officer will be entitled to remain in the employ of Diamond Shamrock and to continue to receive his salary and benefits in effect at that time for a period of 10 years from the date of the execution of the agreement, reduced by the amount of salary and benefits he may receive from another employer. Diamond Shamrock has agreed to pay certain expenses which may be incurred by such officers in enforcing these arrangements.

A ten-year severance contract, triggered by anyone acquiring 25 percent of the stock or by a change in a majority of the board, did seem generous. Now, however, I was negotiating about senior officers' future services with the new owners of the company. I decided to find out Bricker's thoughts. "I have fifteen officers and key managers, exclusive of myself, for whom I want contracts; they include those essential to the continuity of the company and a few who will be 'redundant' after the merger." He offered no objection and did not ask for a list. I pressed forward. "And I will take for my officers the same kind of agreements you have for your officers." He did not hesitate: "Fine." One last item remained. "And I'll take for myself the same deal you have." "OK," he said.

I went back to our consultants. Joe Flom and I reviewed the agreement as it would apply to each of our officers. By the time we got to my contract, we knew we could not follow their contracts precisely. "You're sixty-five," Joe said, "he's fifty-one. The right contract for him may not be right for you." The contracts would have to be individually designed, an issue we would have to raise with Bricker.

We had invited their group to Trader Vic's restaurant for dinner and further discussion that evening. Joe Flom sat across the table from Bill Bricker and presented the matter to him during dinner. We did not yet have a copy of any of their employment contracts. When the papers finally arrived around midnight, we were already at work on our own versions. Bricker's response was that individually designed contracts were fine as long as their total cost did not exceed the cost yielded by Diamond's form. (The final cost of our contracts proved considerably less.)

The contracts were completed during the night. They were cleared with Bricker the next morning and approved with some alterations by the Natomas Board Executive Compensation Committee, all of whose members were outside directors.

My new contract, to become effective on the date of the merger, was to run for six years and six months. In the event that I was terminated or chose to resign after six months following the merger, I would receive a lump-sum severance payment of five times my total annual compensation (calculated from a formula involving base pay, bonus, and employee benefit plans). The severance payment would be reduced proportionately by time worked (and compensation received) beyond those six months.

The agreements for the other executives and managers were similar, but the contracts of individuals essential to the continuity of the business had no voluntary escape clause. A separate agreement applied to Bruce Seaton, who would become president and CEO of the new American President Companies, Ltd. He received a four-year consulting contract with the Natomas subsidiary of Diamond.

The agreements were intended to hold the group together for the transition period, and to provide Diamond with an incentive to evaluate and retain the key managers beyond that time. We knew that we would have no control over Diamond's actions once the merger was effected, but we wanted to protect the people who had managed Natomas, its resources, and its relationships. And I felt that it would be a serious mistake for Diamond to ignore the experience and expertise of our people, and I personally looked forward to working with Natomas's new owners.

· 12 ·

Sayonara

The Natomas Board of Directors met at noon Monday, following the meeting of the Executive Compensation Committee. The lawyers (there must have been fifty at work) had been sending us updates and revised drafts of the proposed Plan and Agreement of Reorganization throughout the day. Although I had conferred with some board members during the week, they came to this meeting unaware that we had reached an agreement the previous evening with Diamond, subject to their approval. Most of the directors arrived not knowing what to expect. They seemed to be pleased that we had reached an agreement, but I knew they greeted the move with very mixed emotions. Douglas McCormack had served on the board for thirty-four years; prior to that his father had been president and CEO of Natomas for twenty-five years. Mortimer Fleishhacker, although only a seven-year veteran, had been preceded on the board by his father and grandfather. Chandler Ide had served Ralph K. Davies as his right arm during the formative years of the modern Natomas, became CEO when Davies died, and had remained as chairman of the board after I became CEO, serving until the previous April, when he had fully retired. I am sure that they, as well as the other more recently elected directors, felt a good deal of nostalgia and regret at the prospect of Natomas's demise as a public company.

Nevertheless, the board seemed receptive. The full board, except for Forrest Shumway, who was in Europe, attended the meeting, along with Joe Flom, Felix Rohatyn, Jim Glanville, and Tully Friedman, among others. Since Forrest was CEO of The Signal Companies, which owned 12.5 percent of the oustanding Natomas shares, Signal was represented by one of its officers.

For some of the board members this was a new experience; others were veterans. But all were extremely concerned with their responsibilities as shareholder representatives and conducted themselves professionally, asking thoughtful and probing questions. Although there are those who disagree, I believe the day has passed when boards of directors of public companies are rubber stamps for management, and certainly not in as critical a situation as reviewing a takeover agreement. Years ago, perhaps, investment bankers and attorneys could conduct a "dog and pony show" to sell directors an agreement they neither understood nor took responsibility for. At one time, the directors of a public company did little more than pick up a fee for attending meetings. But over the past two decades, repeated litigation and a series of court decisions have clearly established the significant responsibility as well as personal liability of directors of public companies. Board members are not required to be experts, but they are required to make reasonable and prudent judgments on the basis of the best advice and counsel they can obtain.

Any large takeover or merger is almost certain to inspire a flurry of lawsuits, many of which are without merit and constitute nothing more than attempts to shake down the company or create enough of a nuisance so that the company will settle out of court rather than go to the expense of defending itself. One of the principal roles of the Skadden,

Arps law firm in our case, for instance, was to guide the directors in carrying out their responsibilities, to counsel them so that they would be as well protected as possible in the event of litigation. In addition to the staff from Skadden, Arps, attorneys from Morrison and Foerster, our own legal department, and each of the investment bankers concerned themselves with forestalling grounds for potential litigation. Diamond Shamrock's legal team was no less imposing. The spin-off of APL and the real estate company would present the Natomas board with special responsibilities. I would later appoint a special committee of outside directors to monitor that transaction; they in turn hired independent outside counsel.

The board met over lunch in the Captain's Cabin. I recounted in detail the events of the week, our mobilization of financial advisors and legal counsel, our evaluation of each of the options for responding to Diamond's offer, and our negotiations and agreement in principle on the previous afternoon. Felix Rohatyn, Joe Flom, and Tully Friedman reviewed their roles and those of their firms, including their efforts to locate white knights and potential purchasers. Both Felix and Joe assured the board that Natomas shareholders were the only constituency whose interests had been considered until we had reached an agreement on the main terms of the proposed merger. They also reviewed their reasons for concluding that, given the circumstances, the agreement in principle was in the best interest of Natomas shareholders.

After lunch, the meeting moved to the Natomas boardroom and continued for another three and a half hours. The principals from the investment banking and law firms were joined by several of their associates and by the investment bankers' counsel. The board examined Diamond Shamrock's management and financial condition, and discussed the financial projections for the new combined company. They also reviewed the new company to be formed from APL and Natomas Real Estate. Questions were raised about Diamond's environmental record, but not all of these received detailed answers; there simply had not been time. Certain questions had to await the results of the due diligence work we would do before the shareholders meeting.

The board was also concerned about the likely future role of Natomas's directors and management. I summarized Bricker's comments but reminded the board that the decisions would be Diamond's once a merger was completed. I repeated Bricker's proposal that the Natomas board continue to function as a board of the subsidiary, but also shared my belief that the board would be phased out within a few months. We knew nothing about management's future other than Bricker's expressed intention to retain the Natomas management to run the subsidiary. For at least the foreseeable future, members of the Natomas management had expressed their willingness to remain with the new company.

After asking the representatives of the investment bankers and their counsel to excuse themselves from the meeting, I reviewed with the board the extent and quality of the work that had been performed by Lazard Frères and Salomon Brothers, and outlined the proposed terms of payment. I had agreed, subject to the board's approval, that each firm would receive $3.5 million for its efforts. These fees, Joe Flom assured the board, were consistent with those paid for such services in recent comparable transactions. After Joe and his associates left the meeting I also reviewed the work of Skadden, Arps and recommended the board approve compensation of up to $1.2 million for that firm's services through the completion of the proposed merger. The board approved both proposals unanimously. The fees were substantial, but the quality of effort was superb. When the stakes are reckoned in multimillion-dollar chips, players cannot afford anything less than the best in professional advice and counsel.

Later, with all the Natomas officers absent, Joe Flom and the Executive Compensation Committee presented the board with the proposed new officers' and managers' employment contracts and explained the circumstances under which they had arisen. The committee's recommendation for approval was unanimously adopted.

The board also considered a series of policies designed to protect the company's employees. The termination policy was amended to reflect the agreement I had reached with Bill Bricker, which would protect our employees for two years after the merger. The company thrift and pension plans were amended to preserve the benefits employees had earned and to make the plans transferable after the merger.

Bill Bricker and I had agreed that Natomas stock options would be exchanged for Diamond stock options or cashed out. Over the years some 140 key officers and employees had been given options to buy a specified number of Natomas shares at the market price on the date the option was granted. The options matured (became exercisable) during the four years following their issue, at a rate of 25 percent each year, and remained exercisable for ten years from the date granted.

Assuming that the value of Natomas stock appreciated over time, employees could purchase the stock at the original option price or elect to realize the difference between the option price and the price on the date of exercise. That difference could be taken either in stock, at the current market price, or in a combination of stock and up to 50 percent cash. For example, if Natomas was selling at $24 and one had a mature option to buy 1,000 shares at $16, one could buy the shares at $16 and hold them, sell them at market, or do whatever any shareholder does with shares. Or, one could elect to receive the $8,000 difference— ($24−$16) × 1,000—as 333 shares or in a combination of up to $4,000 in cash and $4,000 worth (166 shares) of stock.

In June 1983 there were options outstanding for some 1,530,000 shares. The agreement that Bricker and I had reached provided that those options could be converted into Diamond Shamrock stock or cashed out at the difference between the exercise price and a "fair market value" to be determined by the Natomas board. In addition all outstanding options would be accelerated and declared mature, including those issued in 1983. The limitation on cash elections was waived: each option holder could choose to receive in cash the entire difference between the option price and the fair market value of the shares.

Here our investment bankers played a key advisory role. Lazard Frères and Salomon Brothers provided our board with an analysis that estimated the fair market value of Natomas stock at between $28 and $32 a share, based on their projections of the likely total value of 1.05 shares of Diamond stock and one Natomas share interest in the APL spin-off company. The board then selected $30 a share as the reasonable price. (Trading on the stock exchange proved the board right: the market value of the equivalent of one share of Natomas stock in shares of Diamond Shamrock and the new American President Companies on the date of the merger was almost exactly $30.)

The Plan and Agreement of Reorganization, on which the attorneys had been working through Sunday night, led to extensive board discussion. The plan, already incorporating all the major points of agreement, came to more than twenty single-spaced pages. It stipulated that Diamond Shamrock would organize a new parent company, of which each of the former companies would be subsidiaries. William Bricker would become chairman of the board and chief executive officer; both J. Avery Rush, Jr., then vice-chairman of the Diamond board, and I would be named vice-chairmen of the new company's board. Natomas would name four directors, two inside and two outside, to the new board. Each share of Diamond common stock would become a share of common stock in the new company, each share of Natomas stock would be converted to 1.05 shares of stock in the new parent. Diamond and Natomas preferred stock would also be converted to preferred stock in the new company, subject to approval of a majority of holders in each class of preferred stock.

The plan outlined voting procedures for the merger, including the provision that failure to obtain the approval of preferred shareholders would not prevent the merger, and set August 29, 1983, as the earliest date for completion of voting and other necessary transactions. The plan also contained the usual stipulations that neither corporation would make material changes in its companies or issue new stock without consent of the other, that Natomas would not solicit any offers to sell the company or its assets to any other party unless the agreement with Diamond was first terminated, and that each company would grant access to its financial records. Changes in the employee benefit program and stock option plan were outlined. Natomas took responsibility for effecting the APL–real estate spin-off. And both companies agreed to work on behalf of the merger. The document contained, finally, long paragraphs of "boilerplate" (standardized technical stipulations), including provisions for terminating the agreement should the merger not be consummated within one year.

Of particular concern to the board was its responsibility in the event that a third party subsequently made a better offer to Natomas shareholders. But we were assured that as long as the offer had not been solicited by Natomas, the board would be free to consider it. With that understanding, the board approved the Plan and Agreement and directed Natomas's officers to undertake the actions necessary to complete the merger.

The board summarily examined the preparations for the spin-off and seemed satisfied that Bruce Seaton and his staff understood their responsibilities. The board then concluded its agenda with a commendation to the Natomas management "for their tireless and effective efforts and accomplishments culminating in the agreement arrived at between this Company and Diamond Shamrock Corporation."

Later Bill Bricker and his top associates met with the board briefly. Still later that evening the agreement, in final form, was signed by Bricker and me.

Only eight days earlier, I had heard the first word about a tender offer from a *Wall Street Journal* reporter. By Monday night I was too exhausted to appraise the success of our efforts in those eight days. My emotions were mixed. The company with which I had been so closely identified and which had consumed the major part of my energies was, for all practical purposes, under other control. I believed then, and in retrospect am convinced, that we negotiated well. But what of the merger's disruptive effects on employees and the community? Could these somehow have been avoided or reduced? On reflection I think not, but that does not make the contemplation of the consequences any easier.

· 13 ·

Aftermath

On that balmy spring day following the agreement, my associates and I sat in my office looking out over the San Francisco Bay. Diamond's top management had come to discuss the future. The soft music of courtship filled the air. The Diamond officials insisted that they wanted to maintain Natomas as a separate operation, continue its management, and maintain its present board. There was even talk of moving Diamond's international oil operations, far less significant than those of Natomas, to San Francisco. Goodwill overflowed.

I admit to being more than a little skeptical at that time. Natomas's top managers were hardly virgins in the marital bed of corporate marriages—shotgun, arranged, or otherwise. Both Ken Reed and I had been down the aisle several times, on both sides of the transaction. Maintain the present board? Why? With only one shareholder, Diamond, and no public responsibility, it made little sense. Maintain the present management? Unlikely. They needed us until the merger was complete, but after that some, if not all, of us would most likely be viewed as threats to Diamond's present management. Keep Natomas a separate operation? Perhaps. If that met their needs.

The warm summer days between agreement and merger

passed with relatively little friction. The proxy material for the shareholder meeting, voluminous and detailed, was prepared on schedule, and the two sides kept their places.

The only excitement involved a flurry of lawsuits filed on behalf of Natomas's convertible preferred stockholders, trying to force Diamond to redeem the $125 million issue at a premium well above the market. Some arbitrageurs, among others, had bet wrong on the political leverage the preferred shareholders might have. Their claim to the right to a separate and thus blocking vote on the merger had no merit. On August 1, 1983, the Superior Court of California refused to issue a restraining order delaying or preventing the merger.

The activities of the preferred shareholders did, however, lead to one serious confrontation between the companies. Diamond, through Jim Kelley, its general counsel, proposed solving the problem by offering the Natomas preferred shareholders more—but at the sole expense of Natomas common shareholders. I saw that as a violation of our merger agreement and flatly refused; at most, any additional cost should be borne prorata by the common shareholders of both companies. Joe Mandel, Natomas's general counsel, and Kelley debated the matter with increasing irritation. I had conversed often and amicably with Bricker on other matters and sought to straighten it out with him. But suddenly Bricker was not available. Mr. Rush returned my calls. This proved to be a pattern. It was clear that Bricker did not care to deal with confrontation or controversy. From that day forward I neither saw nor heard from Bricker again.

Eventually Diamond backed down and did agree to offer the Natomas convertible preferred shareholders a new Diamond convertible preferred stock with improved terms. This proposal, which was satisfactory from my point of view, was approved at the shareholders meeting in August.

During the interim we had also carried out a due diligence investigation of Diamond Shamrock, a right we had insisted upon in the agreement. (They did not have the reciprocal right for an obvious reason: they were the aggressor.) The investigators did not turn up any material undisclosed liability or other impediment that would have led us to recommend to our shareholders a rejection of the offer. The special shareholders meetings of August 30, 1983, went without incident. The merger was approved.

With the consummation of the merger at the end of August, the courtship ended. The honeymoon was brief. Within hours of the shareholders meetings, Rush, who had presided at the Diamond shareholders meeting in Bricker's absence, advised me that the Board of Directors of Natomas was fired, and I was relieved of my authority and responsibility and replaced as chief executive officer by an executive from Diamond.* Within four months, or shortly thereafter, all but two of the key people for whom we had obtained new or revised contracts in May had been terminated and paid off in full. I had selected Ken Reed and myself as the two inside directors of Diamond Shamrock, but after the merger it was made clear that we were not wanted. Rush asked me to resign as vice-chairman of Diamond, and Ken and I were requested and did resign as directors before attending our first meeting of the new board. Early in 1984 we exercised our right to terminate our contracts and take lump-sum settlements.

The Natomas organization fared no better. The coal and North American oil and gas divisions were discontinued, either through merger into Diamond's corresponding divisions or by sale. Not one executive, administrator, or supervisor from those divisions was kept on. The international

---

*I was subsequently able to persuade Diamond to continue paying our outside directors their monthly fees through April 30, 1984, when they would have stood for reelection.

oil and gas division, exclusive of Indonesia, was moved to Dallas, and the corporate headquarters in San Francisco reduced to a largely housekeeping staff. A year after the merger little of Natomas was left in San Francisco, except the bronze lettered name on the International Building that had served as corporate headquarters. And that too will undoubtedly soon be gone.

The acquisition of Natomas energy assets by Diamond was given mixed-to-negative reviews in the financial press and by the Wall Street analysts, with concern expressed about dilution of earnings and the high level of debt. One can only speculate what they might have said about debt had Diamond's original proposal been accepted.

The Signal Companies, which emerged as the largest single common-stock shareholder of the new Diamond Shamrock Corporation, controlling approximately 6 percent, disposed of their shares through an underwritten secondary offering within two weeks after the merger was completed. Forrest Shumway, Signal's redoubtable chairman, had voted with his feet. Interestingly, Signal retained its shares in the new American President Companies.

Diamond met all its obligations under the written agreement. The executives and key employees whose contracts were terminated were eventually paid in full, though only after a threatened lawsuit when Diamond failed to pay on the agreed-upon date. Nearly all the Natomas employees with stock options elected to receive cash rather than convert to Diamond options; the cost of these elections to Diamond was nearly $15 million. And each of the several hundred salaried employees who were terminated from the various divisions and corporate staff received a six months' lump-sum termination payment, which at least helped them to adjust and seek new employment.

Mergers and acquisitions are invariably accompanied by traumatic changes for the employees of the acquired company. Though the shareholders of an acquired company generally profit, frequently handsomely, many employees find their lives seriously disrupted. Perhaps corporate management's legal mandate to focus on the interests of the shareholders sometimes obscures their vision of the needs of their company's employees.

Fortunately, the spin-off to Natomas shareholders of American President Lines and Natomas Real Estate Company into a new public company, American President Companies, Ltd., proved eminently successful. The market price of the stock soon exceeded expectations, and the corporation's 3,000 employees appeared to feel a certain exhilaration at the prospect of operating as an independent company. The new company recovered from APL's record loss in the first quarter of 1983 and showed a modest profit of $26.4 million for the year. Riding the boom in Pacific trade in 1984, the new company reported record earnings of $103.5 million, nearly double its previous best year.

Reflections

Over a year has elapsed since the merger of Natomas Company and Diamond Shamrock Corporation and the spin-off of American President Companies, Ltd. to the Natomas shareholders, enough time for passions and emotions to subside. I believe I have always had a fair amount of objectivity about the world in which I have lived and labored, but it takes time to regain perspective after a highly charged experience such as the one I have described.

Clearly what occurred was not unique. The corporate world is now awash in tender offers, corporate mergers, and leveraged buyouts, and the trend has accelerated in the last year. The Natomas-Diamond merger, together with the APL spin-off, was the second-largest such corporate transaction in 1983, though it now seems a modest affair compared to the flood of megamergers in 1984 and 1985. How do these corporate machinations affect shareholders, employees, managements, and the communities in which the targeted companies are located? On balance do hostile acquisitions benefit or harm the nation's economy and our society? Is there a better way to respond to the inexorable demands of the investment analysts for quarter-by-quarter growth? Such questions, of course, are not easily answered, but my experience had led me to hold certain conclusions as warranted.

It is my observation that in the majority of successful hostile tender offers there are two winners and two losers. The winners are the management of the aggressor company and the shareholders of the target company. The losers are the management and employees of the target company and the shareholders of the aggressor company. Of course it is never quite that simple. Other winners invariably include the investment bankers and merger lawyers, on both sides of the transaction, and managements of target companies can provide some contractual protection for themselves and their employees and associates. But my generalization is not without validity.

The shareholders of the targeted company, for example, are almost always better off in the short term if the aggressor is successful either in completing its acquisition or in forcing the target company to find another purchaser. This conclusion is self-evident, since the successful aggressor will have offered a premium, usually of at least 50 percent, for the target company's stock. Far less positive, however, is the result for the aggressor company and its shareholders.

In the case of the Diamond-Natomas merger, shareholders who held Natomas as of mid-May 1983 fared well if they sold their new Diamond shares shortly after the merger but kept their American President Companies shares. Natomas stock rose from $15.50 to $18.50 in the two weeks before the tender offer was announced; it closed at $22.50 the day after the tender offer, and at $24.75 the day the agreement to merge with Diamond was announced. Diamond's shareholders did not do so well. Diamond stock closed at $25.00 the day before the tender offer, fell to $24.625 the day of the offer, and slipped steadily to $21.75 on the day the merger agreement was announced.

By August 31, 1983, the day of the merger, Diamond Shamrock stock had recovered to $24.75. At the 1.05-to-1.00 exchange ratio, each Natomas share became worth the equivalent of $25.99 in Diamond shares. Trading of American President shares on the New York Stock Exchange began on September 1, 1983, with a first-day price of $18.875. (For a variety of reasons, we had decided to spin off APL on the basis of one share of the new company for every five shares of Natomas stock.) Each Natomas share was thus worth the equivalent of $3.75 in American President stock, making the total value of the exchange $29.74 per share of Natomas—almost exactly the $30 we had estimated three months earlier.

And American President stock did very well in the months after the company became an independent entity. By the anniversary of the merger, August 31, 1984, its price had risen to $36, or better than $7 for each Natomas share. But Diamond Shamrock stock had fallen to $19.125 by that date. Not all of Diamond's problems, of course, were the result of the merger, but Diamond shareholders were not in a markedly better position a year later than they would have been had they never heard of the Natomas Company. This impression bears out the findings of a study published by *Fortune* in 1982 of the ten largest merger deals of the 1970s.* The study concluded that in the majority of cases the company engineering the takeover either was not notably better off or was worse off afterward. Natomas shareholders who disposed of their Diamond Shamrock stock immediately after the merger appear to have been wise indeed.

In addition to the matter of relative values to the shareholders, a number of other disturbing questions arise. Is

*Arthur M. Louis, "The Bottom Line on Ten Big Mergers," *Fortune*, May 3, 1982, pp. 84–89.

the management of the acquiring company capable of managing the assets of its new acquisition any better or more efficiently than the previous management? In megamergers that involve billions of dollars of assets, is one management likely to be more efficient than two, or perhaps even more, competing management teams? Business is increasingly recognizing that such assumptions as "bigger is always better" no longer hold, if they ever did. In fact, many now agree with economist Barry Stein, "It is clear that, per asset dollar . . . smaller firms are more efficient users of capital."* However true this generalization might be, any ineconomies of consolidation are exacerbated when a company takes over another whose business lies outside its areas of experience and expertise. Perhaps such a recognition motivated Diamond's willingness to let us spin off APL. Even within a single industry, however, a takeover does not necessarily result in better management.

Another troublesome question: Can an acquisition made for cash, whether borrowed or from the company's own resources, be justified when it clearly reduces the resources available to the combined companies for future internal growth? One of the most important goals for most corporations is to increase their equity reserves, but large cash acquisitions substantially reduce equity. The attraction of the ultimate substitution of debt for equity, the leveraged buyout, remains strong: forty such deals were pending or completed in the first half of 1984, for a total purchase price of $11.4 billion, compared with sixteen smaller deals totaling $1.3 billion in the same period a year earlier. But this latest fad, in which a group, usually associated with management, takes a company private by buying up all its outstanding stock with money borrowed against a combination

*Quoted by Kirkpatrick Sale, *Human Scale* (New York: Coward, McCann & Geoghegan, 1980), p. 317.

of assets and cash flow, has already led to excesses and quite probably will result in a new crop of troubled loans.

And the fear of a takeover raid has incited the managements of public corporations to divert significant time and resources to developing preemptive strategies and bulwarks. Surely, such resources and energy could well be better spent improving the company's performance. Ironically, a company's efforts at self-protection can be just the clue that signals vulnerability to a potential aggressor.

The recent trend toward takeovers brings into sharp focus the question of the efficacy and justification of growth by acquisition. At times such a strategy is clearly justified, but acquisition should not be a simple substitute for the far more laborious and less spectacular business of internal growth. Allocating resources and initiating projects whose fruition will take years to realize can offer corporate management none of the excitement and instant ego gratification—heady stuff indeed—afforded by a single successful takeover. But real growth, that is, increased productivity for society as a whole, can be accomplished only by laborious, time-consuming, nonspectacular long-term planning. Corporate America today is littered with the (often barely surviving) remnants of grand acquisition strategies whose failures soon resulted in divestiture, the neat but transparent recognition of a poorly conceived takeover.

However, there is little reason to expect a slackening of the pace of corporate acquisitions in the foreseeable future, unless excesses lead to legislative prohibitions. Perhaps shareholders and boards of directors may become more sophisticated and devise better ways to reward managements for producing internal growth rather than growth by acquisition, but I am not sanguine on that score. The temptation to corporate managers to achieve instant growth through a major acquisition is hard to resist, particularly in the virulently seductive atmosphere created by an army of accomplices—the investment bankers, legal specialists, promoters, and hordes of support groups—who collect hundreds of millions of dollars a year in fees for initiating, aiding, engineering, and resisting takeover maneuvers. No comparable environment exists outside the United States, and I doubt that it will suddenly disappear.

But if acquisition fever will not cool of its own accord, we need stronger regulatory laws. Although I think hostile takeovers are messy and inefficient, I am not in favor of outlawing them, only better regulating them. The dynamism intrinsic to the marketplace eventually does wash out the inefficient and reward the productive. The various securities acts have established basic ground rules for corporate behavior in tender offers, and much has been done to protect shareholders, but more is needed. The regulatory agencies, particularly the SEC, and the ever-alert legal profession provide significant protection against abuse for both the sophisticated investor and the general investing public; yet several abuses persist and deserve attention.

First is the so-called two-tiered merger, precisely the pattern of Diamond's original tender bid, which offered different terms for the 51 percent of the shares it sought and for the remaining 49 percent. Under that tender offer, sophisticated shareholders, including the arbitrageurs, who tendered early would have received $23 in cash for each Natomas share. For those who tendered later or waited for the merger to be completed, Diamond intended to offer 0.92 shares in a weakened new corporation for each Natomas share. But if Diamond reneged on this intention, those stockholders might have been relegated to a minority interest in a Diamond Shamrock subsidiary. In either case, their share value could easily have fallen considerably below $23. Thus, regardless of the waiting periods mandated by present law, the two-tiered merger can result in inequitable treatment of shareholders and therefore puts undue pressure on them to tender before they are able to consider their alternatives. Every shareholder, in my opinion, should receive the same consideration, as was the case in our revised agreement with Diamond. I believe the two-tiered merger should be outlawed.

The stock of asset-rich companies, particularly those in natural resources, usually sells at a price below that which could be realized by liquidating the assets, owing to the higher cost of replacing depletable assets. The current relaxed antitrust environment has provided an opportunity for entrepreneurs skilled in asset evaluation. These corporate buccaneers, more interested in the "fast buck" than corporate growth by acquisition or improved management of the assets, have recently launched various greenmail schemes, and these represent a second area requiring legislative or corporate attention. In greenmail a management buys back at a premium the shares of its corporation from an aggressive shareholder who is threatening to launch a takeover, throw out management, force a sale or liquidation of the company, or initiate a proxy fight for company control. The instigating shareholder may well have purchased the shares with just such a shakedown in mind, but management should not be allowed to use corporate funds to silence the gadfly and protect its own position to the detriment of the company's other shareholders. Managements of public companies should have to deal with the issues on their merits, or if they do purchase company stock from the corporate treasury, they should be required to make the same pro rata offer to all shareholders. Regulatory restrictions or corporation charter amendments that prohibit such purchases would significantly discourage greenmail attempts.

Third, the mandated waiting period, after the tender offer is announced but before shares can be bought up, should be extended to allow target companies to explore their alternatives and defense strategies more fully. Under the current rules, the management of a target company must have sophisticated, up-to-date, and frequently expensive defense mechanisms in place before a sneak attack occurs; otherwise it is likely to fail both its shareholders and itself in achieving the highest value for the company or pursuing the most reasonable alternative course.

Fourth, current policies tend to be inadequate in addressing the dislocation and trauma suffered by employees of a company caught in a takeover. I believe that the boards of directors and managements of both the aggressor and target companies have a responsibility, not necessarily to guarantee jobs but at least to provide financial and professional support for those who are displaced. Responsible managements should provide counseling, job training, and healthy severance benefits in the advent of a takeover, as they do when plants are closed or operations discontinued. All such programs require extensive thought and planning; they cannot be hastily designed in the whirlwind of a takeover. Therefore, I strongly urge all public companies to draft such programs and include them in their corporate defense blueprints.

Fifth, the demise of a major corporate headquarters invariably has a significant impact on the local community, as every large and many smaller cities in the United States have discovered. San Francisco's loss of Natomas may be Dallas's gain, although there is little reason to believe that any increased support Dallas receives will equal San Francisco's loss. A corporate headquarters is the site for major allocations of resources and the residence of the principal corporate officers; corporations are leading contributors to a community's tax rolls and its charitable institutions and activities, such as schools, hospitals, and the arts. The loss of a corporation can be devastating to a community's tax base, development, and culture. Perhaps requiring an environmental impact report that specifically addressed a proposed merger's effect on employees and communities, prior to approval of the transaction, as suggested to me by a thoughtful corporate executive, would supply the needed impetus to a careful consideration of these areas of concern.

Finally, unfriendly mergers and recent developments in the interpretation of antitrust laws have broad repercussions for our society at large. Since the Reagan administration came into office, we have seen a general relaxation of antitrust concerns, of which the abandonment of size as a criterion has been only a part. In the ten years prior to the Reagan administration there were only seven megamergers totaling $14.5 billion, while in 1984 alone there were seventeen such mergers totaling $57 billion. The ease and speed with which megamergers are approved, with seemingly token requirements for divestiture of overlapping or competing operations, raises the strong suspicion that federal antitrust enforcement is now more concerned with satisfying form than substance.

Into this permissive environment rides the modern-day corporate raider, armed with megabucks supplied largely by bankers anxious to improve their own short-term profits. These raiders have frequently met with marked success. Piously parading under the banner of concern for the shareholders of the target company, usually an asset-rich corporation with broad public ownership, they have been successful in forcing mergers or "corporate restructuring"— a euphemism for replacing substantial amounts of equity with debt or effecting other forms of partial liquidation. Admittedly, the net effect has been substantial short-term profits to the target company's shareholders, including, of course, the raider and his associates, and those shareholders whose interest in the company is short-term—the arbitrageurs, the speculators, and the managers of pension and investment funds striving for quarterly performance goals. That can't be all bad, but do the costs outweigh the benefits to the economy and society as a whole?

President Reagan's recent economic report stated that takeovers were *favorable* to the "aggregate income" of the national economy—a statement that I find baffling. Such an assertion can only reflect a short-term perspective that ignores the human and long-term economic implications.

No doubt, some corporations have tired blood, managements that are arrogant or indolent or worse, and the corrective mechanisms afforded by takeovers should not be eliminated or unduly impeded. But from my observation poorly managed corporations have not been the principal takeover targets. Most of the recent major targets have been successful, reasonably or well-managed companies, and invariably rich in natural resources. The rationale is clear: Liquidation, whether partial or total, of assets such as petroleum will under most circumstances produce a higher current price for a resource company's shares than will the stock market, which is affected by dividends and perceptions of growth potential. To stay in business, resource companies must reinvest a substantial part of their cash flow in new production simply to replace the assets they have produced, leading to relatively low price-earnings ratios. This has been compounded by the fact that price-earnings ratios of all companies have declined because of the inflation of the 1970s and high interest rates. The average P-E of the Standard & Poor's 500 is now 11 compared with 18 twenty years ago. With top-rated corporate bonds and government securities yielding 10 to 12 percent compared with 5 to 6 percent, the value of a dollar of corporate earnings has declined while corporate assets have been inflating. Liquidation or the replacement of equity with debt assures that asset replacement will be impaired or eliminated. This can lead only to greater dependence on foreign sources of oil and increased costs to the consumer, who is the ultimate beneficiary or victim of our economic policies.

My conviction is that the activities of corporate raiders and the resulting megamergers and reorganizations are not likely to add to the productive capacity of this nation; most probably they will result in its diminution. Perhaps more important, the disruption in the lives of affected employees and communities will continue to be substantial unless corporate policies or federal law, which now require no more than passing consideration to these constituencies, change. The time may arrive when we not only should consider the shareholders, whoever they may be, since they are already well protected, but also should address the concerns of the people most intimately affected—the employees of the target companies and their communities.

Glossary

(terms as applied to tender offers)

Aggressor   A company attempting an unfriendly takeover of another company.

Arbitrageur   A securities specialist who buys stock of a target company on the hunch that a takeover effort will be successful or will elicit higher bids from the target or from another suitor. Arbitrageurs usually purchase the stock at a price that represents a premium above the market price before the tender offer but that is below the eventual tender offer price. They make money when the tender offer is successful, and lose money if the takeover fails and the market price of the stock falls. The purchase of large amounts of stock by arbitrageurs greatly increases the likelihood that a takeover will be successful.

Board of Directors   Group elected by a corporation's stockholders to govern the company. Directors are frequently nominated by management but are accountable to the stockholders. The directors' duties include naming corporate officers, designating dividends to be distributed to stockholders, and establishing corporate policy.

Book value   The total assets minus debts and other liabilities as listed in a company's records; to be distinguished from the *market value*, the price a company might bring in the open market. In the case of energy companies, book value is often a deceptive indicator, since it is based on the price paid or costs incurred at the time reserves were acquired rather than on their current market value.

Business judgment rule   The standard by which laws hold directors responsible for their actions. The rule requires directors to act "in good faith and in the exercise of honest judgment in the lawful and legitimate furtherance of corporate purposes" (*Auerbach* v. *Bennett*, 47 N.Y.2d 619, 629–31; 393 N.E.2d 994, 999–1000; 419 N.Y.S.2d, 920, 926–27 [1979]).

Chairman of the board   The chairman of the board conducts meetings of the Board of Directors but is not the principal executive officer of the company unless he or she is also the CEO.

Chief executive officer (CEO)   Person hired by the Board of Directors to manage and direct the corporation's activities. The CEO is the principal executive officer, with ultimate responsibility and authority for the corporation.

Common stock   Securities that represent an ownership interest in a corporation. Stockholders share in the company's profits and vote on those corporate decisions that are submitted for their approval under the corporation's charter.

Controlling interest   Ownership of sufficient voting shares (usually at least 51 percent) to control the outcome of votes taken at shareholder meetings, such as the election of members to the Board of Directors. An aggressor's tender offer is usually made for the number of shares it needs of the target company's stock to gain a controlling interest.

Debt   A corporation's final obligations. In a company's records and reports debt is often divided into *current debt*, due within a year, and *long-term debt*, usually in the form of bonds and loans, payable over a longer period.

Debt-to-equity ratio   The relationship between total debt (usually long-term debt) and stockholders' total equity, expressed as a ratio. In general, leveraging a company's equity by borrowing and advantageously investing the funds can benefit the shareholders, but borrowing too much, i.e., too high a debt-to-equity ratio, can leave the company vulnerable to unforeseen negative economic developments.

Dividend The portion of profits that the Board of Directors elects to distribute to shareholders. Dividends are usually paid quarterly and in cash or new shares of stock.

Equity The ownership interest of common and preferred stockholders in a corporation. Equity includes the stated value of common and preferred shares (if any) plus capital and earned surplus.

Full disclosure Federal and state laws and SEC regulations require firms planning to issue or sell stock or to make a tender offer for another corporation's stock disclose all relevant information about themselves and the transaction, including ownership, assets, liabilities, their intentions, and the probable consequences of the transaction for shareholders. Failure to fully disclose constitutes grounds for delaying or halting an unfriendly takeover transaction.

Golden parachute A management contract that provides protection—usually in the form of a severance agreement—to certain of a company's top executives in the event of a hostile takeover. Such contracts should be distinguished from "golden handcuff" contracts, which preserve the integrity and continuity of a company by providing incentives to key managers and executives to remain with the company during the unsettling period when a corporation is under attack or during the transition period after a merger or takeover.

Greenmail The purchase by a company of its own shares at a premium over market price from a troublesome shareholder, usually one threatening to launch a takeover bid or seeking representation on the board.

Holding period The period during which, according to SEC regulations, a company that has made a tender offer is prevented from actually purchasing tendered shares.

Insider trading Buying or selling of securities by persons who, because of their positions, or premature "leaks," have information not yet available to the public or shareholders. Although prohibited by law, insider trading does occur, and the practice has proved to be difficult to control.

Investment bankers Professionals who facilitate financial transactions for corporations, including the issuance of securities to the public or the arrangement of mergers and acquisitions. One or more investment bankers may manage a new issue by helping to set the price, buying securities directly from the offerer, and forming a syndicate with other bankers to sell the securities to the public. In mergers and takeovers, investment bankers provide important advice and counsel to the corporate principals, seek white knights and other alternative offers, and assist in the evaluation of initial and subsequent offers.

Leverage A corporation's use of borrowed capital to increase earnings on its equity. Leverage proves advantageous if the company can earn more on the borrowed funds than the interest it is paying for them.

Leveraged buyout A plan by which a person or group, frequently including the management of a corporation, takes a company private by buying up publicly held stock with funds borrowed against the company's assets and anticipated profits.

Management The officer or officers hired by the Board of Directors to manage and direct the daily operations of the corporation.

Merger The combination of two or more corporations. A merger often involves acquisition of one company's assets by the other, though it can also entail their consolidation into a wholly new entity.

Minority interest The portion of a subsidiary not owned by the controlling company. A minority interest can usually exert only limited influence on the controlling company.

Net income The difference between gross operating income and gross operating expenses after providing for amortization and depreciation of the company's physical facilities and resources and any tax liability on that income.

Operating income The income a business earns from its productive assets and fees charged for its services.

Operating profit The difference between operating income (sales and fees) and the cost of goods and operating expenses.

Outside directors Members of the Board of Directors who are neither officers nor employees of the corporation.

Pac-Man maneuver A strategy in corporate takeover warfare in which the target company makes a counter–tender offer for stock of the aggressor company.

Preferred stock   Preferred stock usually carries a fixed dividend rate and has a preferred claim over common stock in the case of liquidation. Depending upon its issuance provisions, preferred stock may or may not have special voting rights in the event of a proposed merger or sale of the company.

Premium   The amount above market value that is offered for a security. An aggressor's tender offer states the premium it will pay shareholders who choose to tender their stock. Usually this premium is about 50 percent of the stock's current per-share price.

Price-earnings multiple (or **ratio**)   The ratio between the price at which a share of stock is trading and the company's annual earnings per share; a company's price-earnings multiple, usually based on the firm's earnings for the previous year or estimated earnings for the current year, is used by securities analysts to estimate whether the stock is under- or overvalued by the market. A company with a low price-earnings multiple is frequently regarded as a potential takeover candidate.

Proration period   The period in the course of a tender offer during which all shares tendered will be treated equally. If more shares are tendered than the offerer elects to buy, the offerer must purchase the same percentage of shares from each shareholder tendering. This provision was added to securities law to reduce the pressure on shareholders to tender before the target company or other suitors could make alternative offers.

Retainer   An annual payment made to a professional individual or firm to cover future services and to assure the availability of those services.

Saturday Night Special   A tender offer made without forewarning at the beginning of a weekend. The Saturday Night Special is designed to catch a target company by surprise and to put pressure on its shareholders to tender before the target can respond. The Williams Act and subsequent legislation reduce the strategy's effectiveness by extending the minimum time offers must remain open.

Schedule 14D Statement   A document that must be filed with the SEC by a company about to launch or publicly respond to a tender offer. Along with routine information, the Schedule 14D Statement must include the basis on which the company has launched its attack or chosen its response. It is often in a target company's best interests to delay filing for a period of time to prevent the aggressor company from gaining otherwise unavailable information, including its proposed counterattack.

Securities and Exchange Commission (SEC) The Securities and Exchange Commission is a federal government agency, created by the Securities Exchange Act of 1934, that regulates the issuance, sale, and exchange of corporate securities. The members of its Board of Governors are appointed by the President of the United States.

Shark-repellent measures Various tactics, including corporate amendments, used by corporations to make themselves less vulnerable to a hostile takeover.

Spin-off Distribution by a parent company of the controlling stock in a subsidiary corporation to the stockholders of the parent corporation or to the investing public.

Stock option The right to purchase shares at a specified price, regardless of the market price at the time the option is exercised. Stock options are issued to key employees to give them a vested interest in the company's improved performance and earnings.

Suitor An affectionate term for a company that is attempting to acquire a controlling interest in another company. A suitor may be friendly, acting at the encouragement of the target company, or may be an unfriendly aggressor.

Takeover Acquisition of one organization by another, through a cash purchase or exchange of the firms' capital stock. The firm taken over may be dissolved and its assets merged with those of the acquiring firm, or it may be operated as a subsidiary of the new owner.

Target A company that another company is attempting to acquire or control.

Tender offer An offer to purchase shares of a corporation, using cash or securities as payment. An unfriendly tender offer is made directly to shareholders, bypassing management, and most often is the first step toward acquiring control of a company.

Two-tiered offer A tender offer that sets one price for the shares needed by the aggressor to obtain a controlling interest in the target company and another price for the balance of shares to be purchased after control has been gained. This practice puts undue pressure on shareholders to tender during the period of the original offer and creates instability.

White knight A friendly suitor sought by a target company as an alternative to an unfriendly aggressor. The target company seeks a white knight that will offer a price or conditions more favorable to the target, sometimes (but not necessarily) including better future employment prospects for the target's management.

Williams Act Public Law 90-439, enacted July 29, 1968. The Williams Act stipulates various regulations concerning tender offers. The act is intended to protect the target company's shareholders, for example, by ensuring that they will receive complete information before having to decide whether or to whom to tender their securities.

Write-down Reduction of the book value of an asset to adjust for a decline in the asset's market value. For example, a corporation may write down the value of petroleum-producing holdings after the size of estimated remaining reserves has been revised downward.

Index

Designer: Sandy Drooker
Compositor: G & S Typesetters, Inc.
Text: Caledonia
Display: Bodoni
Printer: Vail-Ballou Press
Binder: Vail-Ballou Press